D1113275

Acclaim for
If I'd Known Then
What I Know Now

"I have never read a book that summarizes the basics in life more clearly and accurately than this one. This book should be made available in every school in the U.S.A. I will read this book again and again and will use it as a constant tool to help me through life."

— *Joe Edwards*

"For most of my young adult life, I have asked many people much older and more experienced than me what they would do differently if they could be my age. I was searching for advice that could help me avoid the same mistakes as my elders. I am very fortunate — J. R. Parrish's book, *If I'd Known Then, What I Know Now* has become my guiding light. After reading J. R.'s book and taking it literally, my life has gone from good to great. I have experienced instantaneous results since using J. R.'s advice. I particularly like fulfilling everyone else's need to feel important, which in turn fulfills my needs. On a more personal level, I feel that J. R. Parrish's advice has helped me get on track to achieving my lifelong goals."

— *John Hagerty, golf professional*

"How has our firm managed to survive the last four years with a minimum of scars? I need look no further than to this book sitting on my desk. It is the people. J. R. Parrish built a company based on principles of care, mutual respect, service to others, family, and commitment. Those principles, and others, were never taken lightly by him nor by any of the dozens of us who were mentored by him. They have stuck with us through thick and thin, and they form the foundation of who we are today."

— *Jeff Fredericks, Managing Partner,*
Colliers International

"An attribute of great leaders is their ability to seemingly simplify life's complex problems. J. R. Parrish is a master at this. His humble, down-to-earth, straight-talking style aids in cutting through all of the noise to get to the essence of achieving a successful, harmonious and balanced life. I have been reading the book with my seven-year-old first grader and have already seen a change in her. Every weeknight she can't wait for dinner to be over so we can read the book!

As a student of J. R. Parrish for twenty years, I have seen him positively change the lives of hundreds of people. His company was the envy of the Silicon Valley business community for its extraordinary culture of giving to one another. These same people have better marriages than the norm, and are great parents, daughters and sons who make significant contributions to their communities. These are people who accept responsibility for their actions and lives. Although he spent only one term in college before becoming a milkman, J. R. Parrish has earned a Ph.D. in Human Relations with the publishing of this book (his dissertation)."

— *Scott F. Daugherty, Strategic Realty Advisors*

If I'd Known Then
What I Know Now

If I'd Known Then
What I Know Now

*Why not learn from the | You can't afford to make
mistakes of others? | them all yourself!*

J.R. Parrish

Cypress House

If I'd Known Then What I Know Now
Copyright ©2003 by J. R. Parrish

Cypress House
155 Cypress Street
Fort Bragg, CA 95437
(800) 773-7782
www.cypresshouse.com
Author web site: www.parrishonline.com

Cover design: Gopa and the Bear
Cover illustration: Sandra Lindström
Book design: Cypress House

Library of Congress Cataloging-in-Publication Data

Parrish, J. R., 1943-
    If I'd known then what I know now : why not learn from the
mistakes of others?-- you can't afford to make them all yourself! /
J. R. Parrish.
        p. cm.
    ISBN 1-879384-49-3 (pbk. : alk. paper)
    1. Success--Psychological aspects. 2. Success in children. 3.
Success in adolescence. 4. Success in business. I. Title.
    BF637.S8 P37 2003
    158--dc21   2002011091

First Edition

2 4 6 8 10 9 7 5 3

Printed in Canada

Contents

Foreword

You are about to read a book by one of the most dynamic and successful men you could ever hope to meet. In a few pages, I hope to convey some of the personality of this unique man, a person who can not only talk the talk you'll find in this book, but has walked the walk many times over.

I first met J. R. Parrish at Pasatiempo Golf Course, in Santa Cruz, California, in the summer of 1977. It was my lucky day. By draw I became paired with him, a newcomer to the club, for a Saturday-morning game. I had no idea that he would become a lifelong friend and business associate and the most influential person in my life. I remember wondering, *Who is this charismatic, clean-cut man with the million-dollar smile?* As we walked down the first fairway, I felt his enthusiasm and noted that his attention seemed solely on the others in the foursome, with little concern for himself. I was drawn to him like a pin to a magnet. When he found out that my handicap was eight, his own being about an eighteen at the time, J. R. expressed the hope that someday he could play golf as well as I. (He later became a very accomplished, low-handicap golfer, but that's another story.)

By 1980, I was in J. R.'s office, interviewing to become a broker in his then small Silicon Valley commercial real estate company. This was a huge step for me, as I was in mid-career, with a solid job in a solid company (IBM), but considering completely changing careers to a high-risk, 100 percent commission sales job in a field I knew nothing about. J.R. was someone I wanted to be associated with, someone who can inspire one to believe that he can do most anything. J.R. was sitting behind a magnificent George Washington-style desk in a spotless office with absolutely nothing out of place. His desk shone like it had just been polished. I was later to know that J.R. always kept a spotless desk (even the insides of the drawers were clean and organized), immaculate office, clean and washed car, organized notes, etc. To this day I think one of the reasons he hired me was because I put my coffee cup on the floor rather than on his desk where a ring might have formed.

A year later, J.R. asked me to become president of his company, while he was to remain CEO. J.R. was an excellent administrator, but his first love was always sales, and he wanted to devote his time to developing clients rather than to the company's day-to-day business. So began the most enjoyable and exciting thirteen years of my career (and, I think, his), during which the company grew from a small boutique brokerage to one of the largest and most respected commercial real estate companies in the most dynamic part of the world.

I was with him almost daily, in casual conversations, meetings, sales presentations, private lunches, social events, golf games, and at his monthly "self-improvement" sessions. I give you this background to establish the fact that what I'm going to tell you about J.R. comes from someone privileged to know, observe, admire, and love him like few others.

The first thing about J.R. Parrish that stands out in my mind is his charismatic leadership. Without trying, he's the person in a group who people most want to be near and talk with. He's a wonderful speaker; particularly strong when talking spontaneously and from the heart, in which mode he becomes the most inspirational and motivating person I know. I thought him the perfect CEO: the inspirational leader of the company in both business and moral conduct. There was never a doubt as to who had the last word about the company, yet he allowed me, as his president, almost free reign, and never once criticized or second-guessed my decisions, though I certainly liked to discuss the important ones with him first. He was always supportive both privately and publicly. I looked forward to our monthly company-review meetings, because I knew they would be positive and constructive. J.R. always took the time to write an annual letter of appreciation, which was almost as meaningful to me as my paycheck. Few people are more thoughtful. Over the years, he must have written scores of notes of appreciation to various people (and received as many back). This is what being a leader is all about.

J.R. is the best salesperson I've ever worked with. I mean this in the most positive sense, based not only on my having known and managed many real estate salespeople, but also on having spent fifteen years in sales with IBM at a time when the salesman was "King." He knows sales techniques like the back of his hand, having been schooled in them while at Xerox, but his ability goes well beyond this. First, he will only attempt a sale if he knows in his heart that there'll be a win-win result for both parties. He applies no pressure and maintains an easy, relaxed manner. He always seems to ask the right questions, and exudes self-confidence and integrity. People seem to want to work with and "buy" from J.R. A long-term relationship nearly always results. For example, it was his salesmanship that convinced several nationwide insurance corporations to trust the exclusive leasing and management of their large buildings to a small upstart company, which helped move us into the big leagues. Being a good "salesperson" applies not only to business, but also to many aspects of successful living, from asking for the family car to convincing your spouse that you ought to take that summer vacation. You'll find many keys to being a good "salesperson" in this book.

J. R. is an amazingly focused individual. He sets specific goals and priorities, and then addresses each of them one at a time, evidently able to maintain total concentration on one goal until it's achieved. Many of his goals were directed toward self-improvement. His method is to write his goal every single day in his "day-timer" until he feels it is achieved or internalized. Some examples I recall were "act now," "no criticism," "no gossip," "others," "smile," "seek first to understand, then to be understood," "try praise," "allow time," and "debt-free." By focusing entirely on one goal over a period of time, sometimes months or years, he is able to form the good habits he so desires.

One goal that I particularly remember relates to J. R.'s determination. In 1982, when he was a good, but somewhat ordinary, weekend golfer, he decided that he wanted to become a tournament-contending amateur player. I'm not sure he realized the enormity of the challenge, but, in typical fashion, he set about the task. In effect, he quit working, took lessons, practiced hour after hour, and played golf every day for about a year. He became steadily better, and his handicap lower and lower. His crowning achievement was qualifying to play in the California State Amateur Championships at Pebble Beach in 1983, no mean feat, since qualifiers for this tournament represent the top 100-or-so of several hundred thousand golfers in the state. It was so unusual that it rated an article in the *San Jose Mercury News.* But J. R. came to realize that being a top golfer was nearly a full-time commitment, and that his heart was in his company work, so he came back to his first love. We liked having him back.

J. R. is extremely generous, from both his pocketbook and his heart. I've known him to personally support various salespeople financially if he believed in them. He loves to help good people who work for tips — waiters and waitresses, for example. He learns their names, treats them with friendliness and full respect, and then tips them generously, not to play the role of big shot, but because he genuinely wants deserving people to be amply rewarded for good work. He has assisted young people from outside the company if they were in need and he liked their attitude and potential. Almost always more than just financial, his support included being a mentor. One memorable example was a young aspiring racecar driver, "Memo Gidley." (J.R. also got into open-wheel racing in a serious and successful way—yet another story.) J.R. felt that Gidley had the potential to become a top driver, but he lacked the necessary backing. J.R. fulfilled that need for several years, and even let him drive one of his cars for a full season. Memo has not only succeeded, but has been an Indy Car driver for the past three seasons. Not all of J.R.'s beneficiaries worked out, but the few disappointments didn't deter him for long. He knew he "wore his heart on his sleeve," and expected it to get knocked off once in a while.

Perhaps the most generous and unselfish thing J.R. did over the years was to conduct his "self-improvement" meetings. These were voluntary early-morning (before business hours) meetings, open to anyone in the company. They were well attended; over my thirteen years, I could count on one hand those that I missed. The subject was for the most part "human relations." The basic approach was to go through various books or writings, with J.R. asking various people to read aloud for a time, with group discussion in between. J.R. had a knack of bringing out the relevant feelings and experiences of others without becoming preachy, yet offering his own views and experiences. His recall of other pertinent writings and quotations always amazed me — he loved and studied many of America's founding fathers, for example. Needless to say, much of the culture of his company came as a result of these meetings. On the few occasions that J.R. couldn't attend, these meetings were not the same. He was the leader.

We often wished that we'd been exposed to the ideas we learned in these meetings earlier in life, or that members of our families could share those moments with us. Fortunately, that's what this book is all about. It's one thing to be exposed to ways to improve yourself and your life, and quite another to actually work on them until they become a part of you. That's what J.R. has done and continues to do. He is truly a remarkable man.

Robert E. Babcock

Preface

How many times have you lamented, *"If only I had known then what I know now"?* The purpose of this book is to arm you with knowledge by allowing you to learn from those who have gone before you. The wisest of you will want to learn from the mistakes of others, eliminating much of the pain and suffering inherent in learning by personal experience. Experience is a good teacher, but none of us lives long enough to learn all our lessons by this method alone. The best and least painful way to learn is from the experiences of others, which can make your journey through life less painful and much more rewarding.

An example of what you can learn from others is to be cautious when something looks too good to be true. The experienced person knows that *when something looks too good to be true, it probably is.* Many people, including myself, have lost a great deal of money chasing what appeared to be a great "bargain." I'll tell you about some of those experiences later. This book can be your guide to making better decisions; following its teachings, you can improve your life by minimizing mistakes and taking advantage of situations in ways that reflect an understanding far beyond your years.

The concepts are by no means mine alone; I've been fortunate in having several mentors who taught me principles to live by that contributed to the richness of my life. I've incorporated my thinking with that of my wife, mentors, family, and friends, as well as knowledge I've learned from other sources, including seminars, tapes, and books.

There is an important difference between reading something and internalizing it. Often, when I recommend a book that helped me, the response I get is "I've already read that one." When I ask the person's thoughts on key issues, he or she doesn't remember them, and hardly knows what the book was about. That's fine if you're reading a novel, but if you want the benefits of a self-improvement book, you must go deeper. *When you internalize a book, it becomes a part of you, and you can answer almost any question about its content. The material becomes part of your subconscious, and you begin reacting to situations the way the book taught you to.* I internalize self-improvement books by reading the material several times and writing down the key points. Reading some of the material aloud also helps internalize it.

I asked the people who helped me the most why they had taken their valuable time with me. Each of them told me the very same thing: *"Because you acted on my suggestions."* It became clear that much of my success came from taking literally the people in whom I had confidence. When you have faith in an author, mentor, or friend, the next step is to follow their instructions explicitly. For example, in Og Mandino's *The Greatest Salesman in the World*, the instructions for learning the ten good habits were to read each chapter three times a day for thirty days, the last time each day aloud just before bed. I completed this process twice, and those habits have become my habits. Most people will not be so literal; they might read only once a day, and not every day, and won't read aloud before bed. *Doing exactly as instructed, and promptly, is a big part of the difference between those who succeed and those who fail.*

By taking one of my clients at his word and doing exactly the things he suggested, I received one of the biggest blessings of my life. He became the grandfather I never had and shared knowledge with me that has helped me all my life. I met him through my commercial real estate business when he was eighty years old. Eventually, he invited me to have lunch with him once a week at his home, a tradition that continued until his passing, five years later. I asked him on several occasions, "Why are you so kind to me and helping me so much?" Each time, he told me it was because I took him literally, and promptly did exactly as he suggested. Most people are what he called "Yeah, buts." They ask your advice and then tell you why it won't work. When you make a suggestion, they say something like, "Yeah, but I already tried that and it didn't work," or "Yeah, but that wouldn't work in this case." He said that trying to help such people was like pouring water on a rock—none of it would seep in. I hope this story encourages you to see the value of taking literally the suggestions of those you respect. Learn to act immediately on their recommendations. This trait alone has accounted for much of my success. That wise man must have appreciated my willingness to listen and take him literally, as he bequeathed to me a life estate that has turned out to be worth more than a million dollars.

I've had a lot of help writing this book, and give special thanks to my wife and best friend, Lisa R. Parrish, and to the former president of my company and dear friend, Robert E. Babcock. I appreciate the help and inspiration of Pearl Wible, to whom I taught some of these principles when I was trying out the concept of this book on her fifth-grade class. Others who helped include Donald H. Reimann and his wife Christine Martha, my aunt, Eloise Andrews and her daughter Susan Converse, my son, Ronald Alan Parrish, my daughter, Shirley R. Remington and her husband Michael, my son, James Henri Parrish and his wife Jenifer, my step-mom, Helen Eileen Parrish, my brother, Paul S. Parrish and his wife Pennie, Patricia R. Edwards, Stephen

C. Condrey, Scott F. Daugherty, Richard and Kit Doerr, Donald and Penny Lavoie, Michael and Susan Collier, Craig and Jill Fordyce, Robert and Joan Warmington, Kathy Fleming, André Walewski, Jonathan Anderson, Nicola Opdycke, Daniel Kreindler, Mark and Dawn Zamudio, Rick and Linda Martinez, Scott and Wendy Gaertner, Michael Burke, Dave Schmidt, Stella Rosendin, Diane Gorham, and Bonnie Reimann.

This book would not have been possible without the council of my three mentors: Glenn H. Lay, William Malkason, and Mary Morella.

If I'd Known Then What I Know Now

Overview

You are precisely where you are in life today because of the choices you've made. *It's not your circumstances that determine your success or happiness, but the choices you make in those circumstances.* Two people can experience an identical event, such as a financial disaster, and while one gives up and lives the rest of his or her life unhappy and penniless, the other decides to start over and ends up with more than he had before. This suggests that it's not our circumstances, but how we think about and choose to deal with them that determines the outcome. The information that follows is intended to guide you to making better choices throughout your life.

Before beginning any journey, it's wise to consider it carefully. Walk all the way around it. Before following anyone's advice, it's prudent to ask yourself a few questions: What does the person giving the advice have to gain? What's his track record? What's her background? Since you need to know the answers, I'll share a little of my background with you. That way, you'll get to know me a bit and sense my motivations. I hope you'll conclude that you don't need to have all the breaks to achieve the success and happiness you want.

Born August 1, 1943, I was raised in a small house on a dirt street in Macon, Georgia. I don't remember my mother, who, when I was two years old, left me with my paternal grandmother.

It was just the two of us then, and she provided me a loving environment. When I was seven, I sold flower seeds up and down our street for spending money, and had a paper route at ten. In 1949, when I was six, you could buy a Coke, two glazed donuts, a pack of gum, or any candy bar for only five cents. Gasoline was nineteen cents a gallon, and you could buy a house for less than $7,000.

When I was eleven, my grandmother passed away, and my life would never be the same. I was taken to live with my dad, a chief petty officer in the navy, my stepmother, and three half-brothers. I was taught strict discipline, to do chores, and to share. I received much less attention than I was accustomed to. This did not seem good, but it turned out to be a blessing. During those years, I baby-sat, mowed lawns, and worked at a gas station and a fast-food restaurant. Thanks to the navy lifestyle, we moved coast to coast five times in the next seven years, and I attended three different high schools.

The day I graduated from high school I moved to Fresno, California to attend Fresno State University and play baseball. On the way there I had a tryout with the new Los Angeles Angels, thinking I could make baseball a career. To pay for college I worked for a dairy, getting customers for their home delivery routes. One morning, the man I worked for was killed when a train hit his milk truck. Having no one to take over the milk route, the owner of the dairy asked if I would be interested. At age nineteen, after less than one semester of college, I found myself in the milk business. Six months later, I got married to a wonderful girl who had a beautiful little boy named Ron, whom I adopted. Eleven months later, we had our daughter, Shirley, and five years later, our son, Jimmy. In the meantime, I had gone to work for Producers Dairy in Fresno, California, and was soon put in charge of their twenty-six home delivery routes.

The owner of the dairy had two sons, one of whom would not

come to work for him. There was little teamwork at the dairy, and none of us managers got along very well. In frustration, the owner hired a man named Glenn Lay to come to the dairy to teach us teamwork and to persuade his son to join the company. Glenn had a degree in human relations and was twenty years or more ahead of his time. Most of the old-timers resented Glenn and had no interest in learning from him. In frustration Glenn said to me one day, "These guys aren't open to what I can teach them, but you seem to be. Since I'm going to be here for the next year, *if you'll do exactly what I ask, I'll grow you twenty years in one year."* That was very exciting, so I agreed. He fulfilled his promise, and at the end of one year we both left the dairy.

Addressograph Multigraph Corporation, a Fortune 500 company, then hired me, and after only eighteen months I was their top salesman in the United States and Canada. I had made $12,000 my last year in the milk business, and made $36,000 that year. *I attribute the success Glenn helped me achieve directly to taking him literally and doing precisely what he suggested.* Glenn had me read, study, and internalize two books. Doing what Glenn said and what the books instructed me to do changed my life. Those two books were *Think and Grow Rich,* by Napoleon Hill, and *How to Have Confidence and Power in Dealing with People,* by Les Giblin — two of the most powerful books I've ever read.

Because of my sales success, Xerox Corporation hired me. They had refused to hire me when I left the dairy, because I didn't have a college education. I was so focused on climbing the "ladder of success" that I divorced my wife of seven years. She had been a good wife, but I was a starry-eyed, ambitious young husband who hadn't yet learned the true values of life. I've regretted that decision for many years.

My sales success continued, but I soon became unhappy with corporate life and its lack of flexibility and creativity. I asked myself what I could sell to make lots of money. The best I could come up with was ships, airplanes, or buildings. Ships and planes required technical knowledge that would take years of study, so I decided to go into the commercial real estate business and sell buildings. I got a job with a real estate firm in San Francisco, and soon married a girl I'd met at Xerox. I had become a good salesman, and even though it was a down time in commercial real estate, I was able to surprise my boss and myself by closing eleven deals in the first three months. I had taken the job in October 1973, and in January 1974 my boss asked me to open an office for him in San Jose, California. I had never been to San Jose, but took him up on his offer.

I was successful over the next nine months, though it did take me three months to make my first deal in the new area. I got the shock of my life on October 24, 1974 when my boss walked into my office and questioned me about why I was studying to get my broker's license. He knew that one needed a broker's license to start a real estate firm, and wrongly assumed that this was my motive. The only reason I was getting the license was to further my knowledge of the real estate business, but several of his longtime agents had quit and started their own businesses after getting their broker's licenses. He told me, "Stop pursuing the license or you're out of a job." I'll never forget driving home that night, wondering, *What am I going to do now?*

What appeared to be a great misfortune became one of my biggest blessings. The following Monday morning, I started my own company, using the broker's license of a man I was fortunate to know. By going to night school for several years, I eventually got my own license. The company grew steadily over the next twenty-five years, and I sold it to the employees in 1999.

This is an appropriate place to share with you one of the very important lessons I learned from this experience, which has proven to be true in many instances in my life. *Don't judge the*

If I'd Known Then What I Know Now

*things that happen to you as good or bad at the time they happen.
Just live with them, and in time you'll find that what appeared a
curse might turn out to have been a blessing in disguise. You might
also find that what seemed a blessing turns out to be a curse.*

The reason for much of the company's success was the things
my mentors had taught me. I'll share that wisdom with you
through out this book. Since I had learned the value of effective human relations, I knew my company's success would depend
on treating our people lovingly and honestly. If I looked out
for their best interests, and taught them to do the same for our
customers, we were sure to succeed — and we did. By the time
I sold the company, it had grown to more than 250 people,
$80 million in sales, five offices in the San Francisco Bay Area,
two in Texas, and two in Nevada. I could tell you more about
what happened in those twenty-five years, but I'll interweave
those stories with the lessons, as I'm sure you're eager to get
down to business and so am I.

Three Keys to Success
Regardless of Age

The first key is to recognize the fact that every human being's greatest need, after food, clothing, and shelter, is the need to feel important. By understanding and applying this key to success, you'll put yourself in a position to succeed with people in every aspect of your life. Won't it be nice to know exactly what to do to win with others? Your success and your happiness depend on your ability to get along with others. In his book, *How to Have Confidence and Power in Dealing with People*, Les Giblin makes the point that most failures in the business world are failures in human relations. I can tell you that learning effective human-relations skills completely changed and dramatically improved my life. Since getting along with people is crucial, it's important to learn how to get along early in your life. Human-relations skills should be taught from kindergarten through college.

Your success with everyone you meet will depend on your ability to satisfy his or her need to feel important. How do you feel when someone asks your opinion, lets you go first, gives you the best seat, offers you the last piece of candy, smiles at you, brings you a gift, or sends you a thank-you card? How about when they compliment you, encourage you, praise you, speak well of you in front of others, and show you they need and value you? Does this describe the kind of person you want to be around? These are the behaviors you must emulate if you want to be successful, happy, and popular.

How do you feel when someone interrupts you, mocks you, or frowns at what you say? What if they don't show appreciation for something you did for them, talk down to you, don't listen to you, disregard your opinions, make you feel stupid, or never let you go first? Does this describe the kind of person you want to be around? This is the person you can't afford to be if you want to win with others and succeed.

I'll address the major points for getting along with others, but if you want to read more deeply on the subject, I recommend Les Giblin's *How to Have Confidence and Power in Dealing with People*. It's the best book I've ever read on human relations, and it changed my life.

The second key to success and happiness is your willingness to form good habits. The biggest difference between those who succeed and those who fail lies in their habits. Your habits control you more than anything else does. If you acquire good habits and eliminate your bad ones, you'll succeed beyond your wildest dreams. Everyone is a slave to his habits, good or bad. You see proof of this everywhere that you look. Aren't the spendthrift and the person with poor hygiene slaves to their habits? How about great athletes, musicians, and successful businesspersons? The habits that enslave you include smiling or frowning, being positive or negative, having a good or poor attitude, and being energetic or lazy. *If you're a slave to your habits, and if your habits determine your success or failure, you'd better learn to become a slave to good habits.*

Some of the habits I formed that insured my success and happiness were minimizing debt, maintaining a positive attitude, smiling, letting others go first, and becoming hurry-free.

If I'd Known Then What I Know Now

Additionally, I made my word good regardless of the cost, became meticulous, and learned patience, humility, and how to control my weight. Though I'll cover habits in detail, there's a very easy-to-read book on the subject that changed my life and thousands of others. I highly recommend *The Greatest Salesman in the World*, by Og Mandino — and don't be fooled by the title.

The third key to your success is what I call "The Better World Theory." I call it that because, if you want a better world for yourself, you must stop blaming anyone else and take full responsibility for every aspect of your life. No matter what you're unhappy about, it's up to you if you want it to change. If you want a better world, you must make it so. Start by accepting the fact that *no one else is to blame for your problems.* When you live like this, you gain peace of mind. Any time you blame others for your problems, you're denying responsibility for your own life — and asking for trouble and heartache.

If you start to blame your problems on your spouse, your parents, your friend, or your employer, remember that you're in each of these circumstances by your own choice. Since you made the decision to be in each situation, there is simply no one to blame. Your motto must become *If it's to be, it's up to me.*

I learned the better world theory in 1968, when I was in the milk business. One of our route men was about sixty, and had been at the dairy for thirty years. Frequently, he would have too much to drink and fail to show up for work. On my days off, I'd have to get up at three in the morning to go load his truck and deliver his milk. I soon found myself complaining that the guy was ruining my life. I was told that it was my problem, not his. How could it be *my* problem? It was explained to me that I was in charge, and, inasmuch as one of my men wasn't doing his job, it was up to me to deal with it — or quit complaining. I could fire him, fine him, quit, or let it go, but I couldn't blame him. I resolved the problem by asking him to retire. Now I know that whenever I have a problem, it's up to me to solve it. There's no one else to blame for your problems.

While I'm on the subject of blame, I'll share something I find quite profound. When you implement the better world theory, you eliminate most of the anger from your life. *Nearly all anger distills down to blame.* If you eliminate blame, you begin to eliminate anger. *Anger* is just one letter short of *danger*. The next time you feel angry, stop and ask yourself, "Whom am I blaming"?

Genetics play a role in both your physical and mental health. The chemicals in our brains are not all the same, and our behaviors can vary a great deal. Sometimes, it takes more than willpower to make a desired improvement. Many people can have one drink and be satisfied, while others can't stop until they're drunk. Some people can be moderate in their food intake, but some cannot. If you're among those who can't, it's better to get professional help than to try going it alone.

Before proceeding with the first lesson, I want parents to know that I don't expect your seven-to-fifteen-year-olds to purchase this book. The first lesson is written as a tool for parents. It's a way to open conversation with your children, and a chance to read and discuss the concepts with them. Often, children pay more attention when something said or written by a third party is read or shared with them by their parents. The idea is to give parents a tool to interact with their children on some very important issues. You and your children can discuss the merits of what you read together. Lesson one is designed to open the door to conversations that benefit both parent and child. I have deliberately repeated some things in each of the lessons—especially in lesson one. Repetition is a great key to learning. As I move to future lessons, I'll repeat less.

Lesson One

Ages 7–15

Mom/Dad, Brother/Sister, Friends, Adults/
Grandparents, Manners, School, Your Thoughts,
Habits, The Lesson in a Nutshell, A Few
Profound Thoughts

Overview

The information that follows can help you with life's challenges by arming you with knowledge far beyond your years. These are the ideas I wish I had known when I was your age. By applying these practices, you'll give yourself the opportunity for greater success and happiness than you can imagine today. They will help you get what you want, teach you how to get along better with people of all ages, and help you succeed in many areas of your life.

Let's begin with what I call *"The Have to-Glad to Theory."* There are many things in your life that you simply have to do: bathing, brushing your teeth, doing your homework, and going to bed at a certain time. Since you have to do these things, you might as well learn to do them with a good attitude. Just say, "Have to-Glad to" the next time you find yourself in a "have-to" situation; it'll make it easier on you and everyone else involved.

If I were your age again, I'd make a real effort to avoid arguing and fighting, as they have a negative effect on you and your friends. To be happy and successful you must learn to take actions that have positive effects. To accomplish those positive effects, keep your focus on what is right and good. *Learn now to follow your inner voice.* Everybody has one, and it tells you what's right and wrong for you. By following your inner voice, you'll make better decisions and avoid a lot of pain. *If you find yourself asking, "Is this right or wrong for me?" you can almost always bet it's wrong.* When things are right for you, they usually feel right and you know it. Each time I've failed to listen to my inner voice I've regretted it. Your inner voice will urge you to tell the truth even if it hurts. By always telling the truth, you'll be a standout. If you're truthful only some of the time, how will others know when to believe you? If a friend lies to you once in a while, how will you know when he's telling the truth?

When you find you have fears, learn to overcome them. The way to overcome a fear is to face it straight on. The more you know about something the less you fear it. Knowledge and understanding are keys to overcoming your fears.

Mom and Dad

Dealing with your parents is sometimes very rewarding and sometimes difficult and frustrating. It's good to remind yourself that Mom and Dad brought you into this world, and without them, there would be no you. It's nice being here on Earth, and you're here solely because of your parents. They fed you, clothed you, bathed you, and provided for your every need. You owe your parents a great deal of gratitude for the many years they looked out for you when you couldn't look out for yourself.

Your parents love you and care about your future more than anyone else does. How they treat you is more up to you than you might think. If you show them respect and quickly do the things they ask, they'll be kinder and more respectful to you than if you're rude and fight them on every issue. By adopting the practices on the following list, you can improve your relationship with your parents.

Show Appreciation

Show your parents that you appreciate them for fixing your meals, buying you clothes, giving you a home to live in, driving you places, helping you with your schoolwork, giving you an allowance, and all the other ways they show their love for you. It's a rare child who thanks his or her parents for such privileges. Many young people take their parents for granted. Thank your parents for caring for you and you'll be surprised how much more they'll want to do for you. To appreciate means to increase in value. By showing appreciation, you increase others in value. This is a trademark of successful and happy people.

Be Helpful

Many young people do as little as possible, and often complain about the little they do. To succeed, you want to help as much as possible and never complain. Having good habits will be a key to your success. Helpfulness is an especially good habit. People want to be around others who are helpful, and no one respects laziness. If you clean your own room, take out the trash, and help in the kitchen or yard, you'll set yourself apart. Your life will be much happier and more pleasant than your less ambitious friends'. Parents want to be proud of their sons and daughters, and more importantly, you need to be proud of yourself. When you do things you know you should do, you'll like yourself better, and that's the first step to good self-esteem. Another gift you can give your parents and yourself is simply to stop complaining.

Tell Your Parents You Love Them

Don't wait for your parents to tell you they love you first. They really appreciate knowing you love them, and it's especially rewarding to hear it from you without prompting.

Favorable Behaviors

♦ Smile. Your smile tells other people they're O.K.

♦ Thank your parents and demonstrate appreciation for what they do for you.

♦ Be a helper.

♦ Clean your room without being asked.

♦ Pick up after yourself.

♦ Quickly do the things your parent's request.

♦ Do your homework without being asked or complaining.

♦ Take out the trash, clean up the yard, and help with the dishes.

♦ Feed your pets and clean up after them.

♦ Get enough sleep.

♦ Consider carefully any advice your parents give you.

♦ Go with your mom or dad when requested.

♦ Eat the lunches they pack for you.

♦ Look your parents in the eye when either of you is talking to the other.

- Tell the truth—even if it hurts.

- Laugh a lot.

- Always do what you say you're going to do.

- Say, "excuse me," "I'm sorry," "please," and "thank you."

- Let your parents go first.

- Remember your parents' birthdays and wedding anniversary.

- Close doors behind yourself.

- Rather than just ask for money, ask what you can do to *earn* money.

- After you use something, put it back where you got it.

Unfavorable Behaviors

- Talking back

- Frowning or complaining

- Using your parents' things without permission

- Wearing heavy makeup before it's appropriate

- Cursing

- Watching too much television

- Not doing your homework

- Arguing with your parents (a sure way to lose)

- Fighting with your brothers and sisters

- Staying in bed when your parents ask you to get up

- Playing your music or the TV too loud

- Being selfish

- Trying cigarettes, alcohol, or drugs

- Telling lies

- Being a tattletale

- Bragging

Brother and Sister

Your siblings will probably be the people who stay closest to you and care most about you all your life. The way you treat each other now will have long-lasting effects on your future relationship. Now is the time to truly become friends. Your relationships with your siblings can be among the most rewarding ones you'll ever know. The secret to success with them, as with all people, is determined by how you treat them. Participate in their birthdays and go to their performances. If you love them and treat them with respect now, you'll build a strong foundation.

Have you ever heard the saying *"All I give is given to myself"*? It means that whatever you give to other people, you're also giving to yourself. If you give them smiles, kindness, love, and happy thoughts, they'll give you the same in return. If you give frowns, complaints, and negative thoughts, that's what you'll receive. The reason this concept is so important is because so many people give themselves misery. Get in the habit of thinking of others as well as yourself. *Any time you're thinking of others and doing nice things for them, you're giving yourself a gift at the same time, and insuring yourself a brighter, happier future.* Do things that are in the best interest of your siblings, and treasure and protect them. Be their friend and supporter, and help them any way you can.

Friends

I asked my eighty-four-year-old mentor, "What do you consider the most important thing in life?" He thought about it a few minutes and said, "The friends we have throughout our lives." Your relationship with friends will be one of the most meaningful parts of your life. Make sure to choose your friends wisely. To a degree, you'll become like your friends. They'll have a major impact on your life, so it's wise to choose friends you genuinely admire.

You're fortunate to learn this valuable truth at a young age. It gives you the opportunity to choose friends you can keep for the rest of your life. Imagine when you're in your fifties saying, "I've been friends with Robbie or Candace for forty-three years." Think how close you'll be, the things you'll have shared, and how much you'll relate to each other. Learn now to value friendships, and don't be quick to abandon one. I've heard a friend described as a gift you give yourself. A friend is someone who walks in when everyone else is walking out. Friends look out for each other and don't speak badly about each other. A friend is someone you can count on when the chips are down. Let's take a look at some favorable and unfavorable behaviors for dealing with friends.

Favorable Behaviors with Friends

♦ Treat friends with kindness.

♦ Listen to your friends and don't do all the talking.

♦ Do things your friends want to do.

♦ Ask your friends lots of questions.

♦ Help your friends with their chores.

♦ Be someone your friend can trust.

♦ Learn your friend's birthday and acknowledge it.

♦ Take your friends with you to fun places.

♦ Share some of your favorite things.

♦ Compliment your friends on the things you like about them.

♦ Practice modesty, including not bragging, and dressing appropriately.

♦ Be a good sport, win or lose. You're going to win and lose. Most people are good winners and poor losers. It's a major move to accept your losses and congratulate the winner.

Unfavorable Behaviors with Friends

♦ Making fun of things your friends say or how they look

♦ Interrupting a friend

♦ Changing the subject when your friend wants to talk about something

♦ Being rude to your friends' parents

♦ Arguing or fighting with your friend

♦ Saying anything hurtful behind your friends' backs

♦ Taking credit for something your friend did

♦ Blaming your friend for your problems

♦ Taking more than you give

♦ Thinking of yourself first

♦ Borrowing and not paying back

♦ Stealing or lying

Adults and Grandparents

The earlier you learn to deal effectively with adults, the more success and happiness you can expect. Your answers to the following questions will show you why. Who has lived a long time and had experiences that can be helpful to you? Who is far ahead of you financially? Who has time on their hands, and remembers when they were young, and would like to help a young person succeed? Who has greater love than your grandparents have?

It will help you to remind yourself each day that *much of your success in life depends on your ability to get along with others.* Besides your parents, the people who can teach and help you the most are your grandparents and other adults. How can you make a good impression and make them want to help you? Now is a good time for you to learn how to make a good impression on anyone. *First impressions are lasting, and you never get a second chance to make a good first impression.* If you make a good first impression, you can do a lot wrong after that and the other person will still think well of you. If you make a bad first impression, it's difficult to change people's minds, no matter how you conduct yourself from then on. Clearly, making your first impression a good one will benefit you, and I'd bet you'll be surprised how it's done.

The way to make a good first impression is to show other people that you are impressed with them!

Here are some of the best ways to impress others:

♦ Listen carefully to them and ask questions about what they say.

♦ Stay on their subject.

♦ Agree with them every time you can.

♦ Look them in the eye.

♦ Ask for their advice, and repeat some of their words to show you're paying attention.

♦ Offer to shake hands as soon as you are introduced and make it a firm handshake.

♦ Use their names, and call them *Mr.* or *Mrs.* or *Ms.* if they are much older than you are.

♦ Stand when they enter or exit the room.

♦ Smile a lot.

Favorable Behaviors:

♦ Let adults go first.

♦ Offer your seat when needed.

♦ Use their name.

♦ Call them *Mr.* or *Ms.* or *Mrs.* until they ask you to use their first name.

♦ Always say "please" and "thank you."

♦ Ask questions of adults, and listen to what they have to say.

♦ Try what they suggest.

♦ Be respectful and not loud.

♦ Help them in situations that require physical ability.

♦ Ask them about their lives.

Unfavorable Behaviors:

♦ Making too much noise

♦ Creating chaos

♦ Talking too loudly

♦ Interrupting

♦ Running and jumping around in their home

♦ Acting like a smart aleck

♦ Talking back

♦ Frowning

♦ Arguing

Manners

One purpose of good manners is to open up social situations for you. If you want to get along well with others and have them respect you, good manners are a must. Good manners are like a pretty picture that everyone wants to look at, while bad ones are like a dirty rag that no one wants to touch. Good manners will attract people, open doors, and give you the opportunity to have and do things not available to those without them. Good manners aren't hard to develop, and once you have them as a habit they're yours for life.

Good Manners

♦ Smile: It tells others they're doing well. Be sure to make smiling a habit.

♦ Say "please" and "thank you."

♦ Let others go first.

♦ Get permission before using something that's not yours.

♦ Eat with your mouth closed and your elbows off the table.

♦ Be quiet and listen when someone else is talking.

♦ Say you're sorry when you do something wrong—and mean it.

♦ Say, "Excuse me" if you must interrupt.

♦ Always pick up after yourself.

♦ Refrain from running, jumping, or throwing things in the house.

♦ Eat and drink slowly, without gulping or slurping.

♦ Don't interrupt the conversation of others.

♦ Call those much older than you *Mr.* or *Mrs.* or *Ms.* until they tell you otherwise.

♦ Ask, "May I?" rather than "Can I?"

♦ Pay sincere compliments.

♦ Control your urge to talk back.

♦ Resist the temptation to talk behind someone's back.

♦ Look at people when talking to them or when they're talking to you.

♦ Never use bad language.

♦ Stand when a woman enters the room.

♦ Stand up to shake hands with anyone.

♦ Don't talk with food in your mouth.

♦ Use your napkin, and don't use your clothes as a napkin.

School

Since you're going to spend twelve to sixteen years in school, you should give it your best effort. Going to school is a privilege, not something to be taken for granted. When you're older you'll regret it if you don't make the most of this opportunity. School will probably be the only time in your life when you'll have the opportunity to just sit and learn all day with few other responsibilities. Americans are extremely fortunate to be given an education. Wise parents will teach their children how important school is from the very outset.

Your teachers are in a position to help you, and smart students realize the value of getting along with their teachers. The way to get along is by using the same skills you learned in dealing with your parents, other adults, and your siblings: the first step is to make a good first impression; the second is to make your teachers feel important.

School offers opportunities to make good friends, learn many new things, and participate in diverse activities. It's a great place to learn a foreign language, learn to play a musical instrument, or participate in your favorite sport. You might want to try several sports, as they teach you about teamwork, commitment, and discipline. Learn to read and enjoy books as early as possible. School is also a place for you to learn and practice your social skills, which will be tremendously important when you begin your career.

Seize the opportunity to learn, and to spend time with people who've accomplished what you want to, because they'll challenge you, and that's the way you can grow the most. Never be afraid to ask what you don't know.

Your Thoughts

You will become what you think about. Your thoughts are a preview of your future. You either take control of your thoughts, or they will control you.

Good thoughts bring about good results, and bad thoughts bad results. If you watch a movie, a television program, or read a book that's full of love, you fill your mind with love, and that helps you become a more loving person. If you fill your mind with hate, it will show up in your life. The same can be said for success instead of failure, happiness instead of sadness, good instead of bad, and right instead of wrong. Since you become what you think about, it's wise to think about what you *want* to become. The first step to any goal is thinking about it. Filling your mind with healthy thoughts will serve you well, and the more you control your thoughts, the easier it is to become what you want to be. It's essential to learn to think for yourself and realize that there are always consequences for what you think about. Be sure to distinguish between *your thoughts* and the things that can influence your thinking, such as movies, music, television and friends.

One hot summer's day when I was ten years old, I began thinking that I wanted one of those huge bottles of Coke. I had no money, but kept thinking how much I wanted that Coke. I let my thoughts get the best of me, and decided I would just go in the store and sneak out with one. I knew this was wrong, but let my desire control me.

Surprisingly, I made it outside without getting caught. This was long before twist-off caps, and I had no opener. I tried everything I could to open that bottle, but nothing worked. Frustrated, I decided to break the top off the bottle by hitting it against a brick pillar. As I did, the bottle exploded and the glass blew a hole in my hand—right down to the bone. I'm telling you this to help you understand that *thoughts are things,* and you'd better be careful what you think about.

The other reason for sharing this story is to have you learn that you can't do wrong without paying the price. Every action, whether good or bad, has consequences. Sometimes, they're instant, like what happened to me; other times, it might take years, but you'll pay for doing wrong. I had to get many stitches in my hand and it was very painful. Follow your conscience and always do what your inner voice tells you. Each time I've ignored my inner voice, I've paid a high price. The Scout Law goes a long way toward keeping you on track. "A scout is trustworthy, loyal, helpful, friendly, courteous, kind, obedient, cheerful, thrifty, brave, clean, and reverent."

Habits

The difference between those who succeed and those who fail lies in their habits. Good habits can unlock the door to success and happiness for you. Let's look at some favorable ones:

♦ Brush your teeth twice each day.

♦ Pick up after yourself.

♦ Show respect to adults.

♦ Make your bed as soon as you get up.

♦ Help with the dishes and take out the trash.

♦ Smile and laugh a lot.

♦ Be honest, kind, thoughtful, and helpful.

♦ Do your homework, and do the best you can.

♦ Earn your own spending money.

♦ Finish what you start.

♦ Always tell the truth.

♦ Set Goals. There are three rules for goal setting: your goal must be believable to you; you must put it in writing; and you must set a specific time to accomplish it.

Another habit I want to cover with you is temper. Having a hot temper is a very bad habit and can cause you problems all your life. There's no place for ill temper in a happy life.

There was a young man who had a bad temper. His father gave him a bag of nails and told him that every time he lost his temper, he must hammer a nail into their backyard fence. The first day, he drove thirty-seven nails into it. Over the next few weeks, as he learned to control his anger, the number of nails he hammered each day gradually dwindled. He discovered it was easier to hold his temper than to drive those nails into the fence. Finally, the day came when the boy didn't lose his temper at all. He told his father about it, and the father suggested that the boy now pull out one nail for each day he was able to control his temper.

The days passed and the boy was finally able to tell his father that all the nails were gone. The father led him to the fence and said, "You've done well, my son, but look at the holes in the fence. The fence will never be the same. When you say things in anger, they leave a scar just like this one. You can put a knife in a man and draw it out, but no matter how many times you say

'I'm sorry,' the wound remains."

A verbal wound can be as bad as a physical one. Bad tempers lead to many verbal wounds.

The Lesson in a Nutshell

♦ Have to-glad to: If you have to do anything, learn to do it gladly.

♦ Show respect to your parents, and listen to them.

♦ Review the lists of favorable and unfavorable behaviors.

♦ Be especially kind and thoughtful to your brothers and sisters.

♦ Cherish your friendships, and practice being a good friend.

♦ Show respect to adults, and remember that they can help you.

♦ Your manners will greatly influence your success and happiness.

♦ Learn all you can in school. Respect your teachers and do your best.

♦ Your thoughts are a preview of your life's coming attractions.

♦ Your habits will determine the difference between your success and failure.

♦ Your success depends largely on your ability to get along with others.

A Few Profound Thoughts

♦ Listen carefully to your inner voice; going against it will lead to problems.

♦ Never say anything about yourself that you don't want to be true.

♦ Admit mistakes quickly. Most people try hard to cover them up.

♦ We are controlled by what we do repeatedly (habits).

♦ If you think you can, you can, and if you think you can't, you can't.

♦ Appreciative words are one of the most powerful forces for good on Earth.

♦ Listen to what others have to say, then make your own decisions.

♦ You've got to have a dream if you want to make a dream come true.

♦ There's no place to hide a sin, without your conscience looking in.

♦ A dog is such a lovable animal because it wags its tail instead of its tongue.

♦ A whale is only harpooned when it's spouting. Be careful what you say.

♦ A diamond is a piece of coal that stuck to the job.

If I'd Known Then What I Know Now

Lesson Two

Ages 16–25

Family, Others, Dating/Marriage, School, Career, Finance, Health, Your Thoughts, Habits, The Lesson in a Nutshell, A Few Profound Thoughts

Overview

You're now entering one of the most exciting times in life. Even though you probably felt quite grown up at thirteen, many young people think they've got it entirely figured out between sixteen and twenty. This is often the time when your parents seem to have lost it, and you have found it. Believe me, nothing could be farther from the truth. These are truly critical years that can make or break your future.

Even though every phase of your life is important, none of them is quite as critical to your future as this one. It's during this period that you set the foundation for the way the rest of your life is likely to turn out. Now you'll start thinking for yourself and putting in place the habits that will determine your fate. You'll grow from adolescence to adulthood, and the choices you make will have lasting effects. It's very important for you to get on the right track during these years, and the following information is designed to help you.

***Your future will depend on
your answers to these questions:***

♦ Will you listen to those who have been where you're going?

♦ Will you surround yourself with the right people?

♦ Will you study hard and truly do your best?

♦ Will you date the right people and for the right reasons?

♦ Will you keep a good and positive attitude?

♦ Will you form good habits?

♦ Will you control your thinking?

At this point it's a must for you to understand and put into practice *the Better World theory.* Simply stated, you and you alone are responsible for your life. Your success or happiness is entirely in your own hands. There's no one to blame for anything you don't like about your life, and if you want your life to be different, it's up to you to change it. To take control of your life and get the results you want, you'll need to become an expert in dealing with people. Winning with people starts with making a good impression, so let's review first impressions.

You never get a second chance to make a good first impression. First impressions are lasting impressions. Don't you find that you're slow to change your first impression? Since this is how most people are, it's vital to make sure your first impression is a good one. Making a good first impression is particularly significant when you're meeting a new teacher, applying for a job, or going out for a team and meeting the coach for the first time.

How do you make a good first impression? Most people think it's by dressing well, showing how smart they are, or something else about themselves. The way to make a good first impression is to *show other people you're impressed with them.* It's important to smile, dress nicely, and be polite, but the way to impress people is by letting them know that they've impressed you. You're sure to make the wrong impression by boasting or talking about yourself. It's important to be yourself; your true colors will come out soon enough, so don't fake anything. Talk about them, ask them questions about the things they say, pay them sincere compliments, and look them in the eye. Show all the approval you can for the things people do, say, and wear. Tell them all the ways that you're like them, and make notes of some of the things they say. They'll go away thinking you're one of the brightest people they've ever met.

As you begin to deal with life as an adult, you'll need to solve a variety of problems. Learning to deal effectively with them now will put you miles ahead of the pack. One challenge will be figuring out which problem to deal with first. Here's a story that will help you solve problems:

A teacher stood before his students and told them it was time for a quiz. He pulled out a wide-mouthed, one-gallon Mason jar and set it on a table. Then he produced about a dozen fist-sized rocks and carefully placed them, one at a time, into the jar. When it was filled to the top and no more rocks would fit inside, he asked, "Is this jar full?" Everyone said yes. He reached under the table and pulled out a bucket of gravel. Then he dumped some gravel in and shook the jar, causing bits of gravel to work themselves down into the spaces between the big rocks. Then he asked the group again, "Is the jar full?" "Probably not," one of them answered.

He brought out a bucket of sand. He started dumping the sand in, and it went into all the spaces left between the rocks and the gravel. Once more he asked, "Is this jar full?" Then he grabbed a pitcher of water and began to pour it in until the jar was filled to the brim. Then he looked up at the class and asked, "What's the point of this exercise?" One eager beaver raised his hand and said, "The point is, no matter how full your schedule is, if you try really hard, you can always fit some more into it!"

"No," the teacher replied, "that's not the point. The truth this teaches us is that *if you don't put the big rocks in first, you'll never get them in.*" Examples of this might be finishing school or learning to tell the truth. What are the "big rocks" in your life? Be sure to deal with them first.

I'll cover many of the key ingredients for success in this chapter. Just reading them won't insure your success. Knowledge isn't the same thing as wisdom. *Wisdom is knowledge put into practice.* The first step is learning, but it's of no value unless you apply that knowledge. To know and not to do is not to know.

Family

Good advice is not always peaches and cream—that's why so few people follow it. This period of your life is an especially important time to listen to the advice of your parents. They have lots of experience with the issues you're experiencing for the first time, and they have your best interests at heart. It's easy to follow their advice when they're telling you what you want to hear, but the real test comes when they're cautioning you about something you don't want to hear.

When, at age nineteen, I decided to get married, my dad gave me good reasons why it wasn't a good idea. I was blinded by my desires and didn't listen to him. There's no question that he was right and was trying to look out for me. If I'd known then what I know now, I would have asked my parents a lot more questions. When they gave me answers I didn't like,

I'd have listened carefully to their reasoning. The time to really listen is when you're getting an answer you don't want. You'll usually find there's a good reason for what they're saying, and save yourself a lot of heartache by following their advice. Parents rarely have anything to gain by what they're telling you. When someone who has nothing to gain from it offers you advice, they're looking out for your best interests. Think back to how advice your parents gave you turned out, whether you followed it or not. It's likely you'll come out better by listening to their advice. A very wise man once told me, *"He is not a friend who always makes you laugh, but he who sometimes makes you cry."*

If I'd known then what I know now, I wouldn't have argued with my parents. By "arguing" I mean raising my voice, pouting, or glaring. Instead of contradicting them, I would first try to understand where they're coming from and why. I'd show much more appreciation for all they provided for me. I'd hug them more often, and show and tell them that I loved them. I'd do what they asked of me right away, and not have to be asked twice. I'd help them more around the house. If you treat your parents with respect you'll be surprised how much more respect you get from them. To be soft-spoken, kind, and gentle with your parents will serve you well. They deserve it, and you'll have fewer regrets when you grow older. Look down the road a few years; consider how you'll want your children to treat you, and treat your parents that way today.

No discussion of family would be complete without giving thought to people raised under special circumstances. I'm using this term to describe single-parent homes, and homes where a stepparent or relatives are raising children. Many young people blame their unhappy circumstances on the way they were raised. No matter how you were raised, you must take control of your life at some point; when you do, there's no longer anyone to blame. To have good mental health you have to accept responsibility for every aspect of your life. It's time to forget about the past and move on with your future. Blame only makes you look bad and delays your progress. Psychologists tell us that one measure of good mental health is to appreciate what you have, learn to forgive, and find the good wherever you go. Your background might have influenced who you are, but you are responsible for who you become.

Several years ago, an important speaker arrived to address the student body of a small South Carolina college. The auditorium was filled with students excited about the opportunity to hear a person of her stature speak. After the governor introduced her, the speaker moved to the microphone, looked at the audience, and began: "I was born to a mother who was deaf and could not speak. I don't know who my father was. My first job was in a cotton field." The audience was spellbound. *"Nothing has to remain the way it is, if that's not the way a person wants it to be,"* she continued. "It's not luck and it's not circumstances and it's not being born a certain way that makes a person's future become what it becomes." And she softly repeated, "Nothing has to remain the way it is, if that's not the way a person wants it to be. *All a person has to do to change a situation that brings unhappiness or dissatisfaction is answer the question, How do I want this situation to be? Then the person must commit totally to personal actions that carry them there."* Then, her beautiful smile shone forth as she said, "My name is Azie Taylor Morton. I stand before you today as treasurer of the United States of America."

It's a shame our own parents couldn't raise all of us. It would be even better if we were all raised with lots of love and taught all the right things, but that's a far cry from reality. Many of the most successful people on Earth were raised in special circumstances. If you happen to be one of us, find the good in your situation, and make your life turn out the way you want it.

Others

You're living at a very complex time, when virtually nothing is simple. Learning the virtue of simplicity can bring you a great deal of peace. Many years ago, I began wondering if there might be one word that led to success and happiness. I was trying to distill life down to one simple word that had brought others success and could do the same for me. I had already learned many things that worked well for me:

♦ Small attempts repeated will complete any undertaking.

♦ You reap what you sow, and you get what you deserve.

♦ It's whom you know as much as what you know.

One day, the word finally came to me, and hit me like a ton of bricks. I knew I had discovered something special. Immediately, I had a plaque made with the word on it and displayed it prominently in my office. Today, it's a license plate on our car and the name of our golf cart, and my daughter Shirley had it written on a huge rock we keep on our front porch. All of these constantly remind me that the secret to a successful and happy life is *"Others."*

When you put your focus on others, good things will begin to happen to you. Consider the people you like and respect the most, and I'd bet you'll find that thinking of others is one of their strong points. The truth is, our entire lives depend on others. Who grows your food, and builds your home and car and all that goes with them? Who picks up your trash, treats your medical and dental problems, makes your clothes, and pilots the planes you fly in? Once I realized our need for interdependence, I made it a priority to focus on others. My life changed for the better from that day forward. This is one of the most important principles for success and happiness.

"All I give is given to myself." Those seven words can make it much easier for you to think of others. What you do for others you also do for yourself. How you treat others is also how you are treating yourself. When you're greedy, selfish, or rude to others, you are giving the same to yourself. When you give love, smiles, approval, and acceptance to others, you give them to yourself at the same time. What's the reason your favorite teacher, grandparent, or friend is your favorite? It's because they think of you, not just of themselves. It's natural to look out for yourself and think about your own best interests. Thinking of others doesn't necessarily come naturally, especially when you're young. It's something you have to think about and practice until it becomes a habit. A good way to make it a habit is to write the word *others* somewhere that you'll look at it daily. Then ask yourself each day, *What have I done for others?* Thinking of others means thanking them for the smallest things they do for you and remembering anyone who has been kind to you. Make this a habit now and your chances for success and happiness will be multiplied greatly.

One way to attract and win with others is to learn the triple-A formula for success. The three A's stand for Acceptance, Approval, and Appreciation. *Successful people are successful because they're willing to do the things unsuccessful people are unwilling to do.*

Acceptance: Don't you want to be accepted as you are? Don't you want to be around people who allow you to relax and let your hair down? You win with others when you give them the right to be themselves. If you accept them as they are, you'll be revered. A good way to start practicing acceptance is by accepting people regardless of their race, religion, or political preferences. This is the essence of a live-and-let-live philosophy. When you begin accepting others as they are, you'll be pleasantly surprised at how they begin to accept you as you are. Acceptance is a blessing to both giver and receiver.

Approval: Approval goes farther than acceptance. It means finding things you like about someone. Approval has the most impact when it's not the obvious. To tell a beautiful woman she's beautiful is the obvious; however, to notice and compliment her on her sense of humor is much more powerful. Look for things you can approve in others and let them know about it. One sure way to lose with people is by showing disapproval. Practice approval and watch how people warm up to you.

Appreciation: Appreciation means to increase in value. When you show appreciation to people, you raise them in value. Thank people, notice people, and treat them as special. Kneel down to eye level when talking to a child, and show your appreciation through your smile. Be sure to remember and acknowledge any nice thing a person does for you. Showing appreciation is one of the secrets to an attractive personality.

A wise man told me that the answer to a lot of our questions could be found by looking to nature. He said, "Just open your windows, look out side to see how nature operates, and you can learn a lot."

Looking to Nature

In the fall when you see geese heading south for the winter, flying along in "V" formation, you might be interested to know what science has discovered about why they fly that way. As each bird flaps its wings it creates uplift for the bird immediately following. By flying in a "V" formation, the whole flock gains at least 71 percent greater flying range than if each bird flew on its own.

People who share a common goal and work together as a team can get where they want to go quicker and easier than those who try to go it alone.

Whenever a goose falls out of formation, it suddenly feels the drag and resistance of trying to fly alone and quickly gets back into formation to take advantage of the lifting power of the bird immediately in front.

If you stay in formation with those who are headed in the same direction you want to go, it will pay off.

When the lead goose gets tired it rotates back and another goose flies point.

We should take turns when doing hard jobs.

When a goose gets sick, or is wounded, and falls out of formation, two others fall out with it and follow it down to help and protect. They stay with it until it's either able to fly or until it dies.

We need to learn to stand by each other when times require it.

Dating / Marriage

Overview

As you go through life, a few really big decisions impact your future for many years, and one of them is marriage. If you get marriage right it can be the best decision of your life, but get it wrong and it can cause massive misery. There's probably nothing else that can create as much happiness for you as finding the right mate. From personal experience and the research I've done, I know one of the keys to getting it right: *The person you choose must be and remain your very best friend.*

Many young people date and marry for the wrong reasons. When you're choosing someone to date, take a close look at the kind of person they are down deep. Do they share your values? Are they thoughtful, kind, considerate, loving, gentle, honest, fair, giving, happy, and fun? If so, you're likely on the right track. If they're negative, selfish, unhappy, unkind, rude, crude, mean, conceited, hateful, rough, or dishonest, you're asking for trouble. Even *one* of those negative traits is reason for concern. By the same token, it's important to realize that no one's perfect. There will always be some faults or traits you may not find appealing about someone. The trick is to let go of the ones you can accept.

When thinking of dating and marriage it will serve you well to realize you're not going to change the other person. You want to be who you are and so do they. Too many people go into relationships thinking they love someone—except for a few things that they'll get them to change. Maybe they're exceedingly jealous or selfish and those things worry you. Remember that those are deep-seeded traits, and reflect who that person really is. You can bank on the fact that his or her current behavior will be the best they have to offer, as we're all on our best behavior when dating. If something bothers you, it's wise to put all your cards on the table from the start. Ask yourself, *If he never changes, can I live with it?* If not, move on, unless he shows you he wants to change and you see progress. A great concept for life is *live and let live.* You be yourself and let all others do the same. If you both want to work together to improve, you're on your way. Being stuck in your ways will eventually lead to trouble. An open mind is a healthy mind, and flexibility is a virtue in building and maintaining relationships.

Dating

Dating can be a time of great fun and excitement. Don't be fooled by the seeming simplicity of the following material. I deliberately keep things simple and understandable to help you make dating a wonderful, rewarding experience. Dating is getting to know someone on a very personal basis. It's a little like shopping, or like trying different kinds of foods to see which you like most and why. When you go on a date with someone for the first time, it's best to take it slowly. The first few dates may be more enjoyable if they're during the day and other people are around.

Any discussion on dating or marriage should begin with how differently men and women think and act. This is an area where I particularly wish I'd known then what I know now. The differences between men and women have been a topic of conversation and confusion for eons. John Gray, Ph.D wrote a book a few years ago that I consider a treasure on this subject. It's very informative and interesting, and will help you at any stage of life. It's called *Men are from Mars, Women are from Venus: A Practical Guide for Improving Communications and Getting What You Want in Your Relationships.* It's very enjoyable reading, and provides great insights that will help you with the dating process. I'll cover some of its concepts in this lesson.

Here are some examples of the differences in men and women's thinking:

Often, when a woman brings up what appears to be a problem, she's not looking for a solution, but simply wants to express her self. This is a foreign concept to most men, who go into a problem-solving mode given any opportunity. Men are very quick to provide unwanted solutions to a woman who wants only to be heard.

When there's tension in the air, women often want to talk about it immediately and in detail. Men generally want to get away and think about it alone.

A shocker is the difference between how men and women keep score: If a woman does something really big for a man, she gets lots of points that can last a month or two. With a woman, a man gets one point at a time regardless of the act; buy her a special gift or empty the dishwasher—and get one point.

Dating is a prerequisite for marriage. Young people shouldn't consider getting married until they're about twenty- five. Even that's young for a man, since men generally mature later than women. I recommend that a woman of about twenty-five marry a man of about thirty-five for them to have the best chance for success.

Your hormones are at an all-time high during the dating years. Feelings are important and real, but logic is much more reliable and safe. Please keep in mind that no matter how hot and steamy a relationship may be at first, that part will fade and there'd better be something more to take its place. The only reliable thing that can is friendship.

Perhaps you've heard that *beauty is only skin deep.* There's much more truth to that statement than meets the eye. Regardless of your gender, you'll want someone to cherish you and treat you with love, kindness, and respect. People obsessed with looks are often self-centered and might not be the best ones to date. They tend to look out for and think about themselves and not you. I'm not speaking of people who are good looking, but people who are obsessed with how they look. It's natural to want someone who's attractive, but don't let that override your good judgment. In the long run, you'll be more concerned with how they treat you, than how they look. Interestingly, the better they treat you, the better they'll look to you. Let's take a look at dating in terms of favorable and non-favorable behaviors.

Favorable Behavior for Young Men

Smile At Her A Lot
Your smile makes her feel good and signals your approval. People are drawn to people who smile, while frowns cause concern and put a damper on life.

Be On Time
This trait of winners tells her she's important and that you take her seriously.

Show Respect for Her Family
When you meet her parents, be quick to smile, look them in the eye, extend your hand, and introduce yourself. Tell them some of the things you like about their daughter and why. Call them *Mr.* and *Mrs.* until they invite you to call them by their first names. Get her home on time after a date.

Treat Her As Precious
As a rule, young women are more sensitive than guys and need to be treated as such. Girls go to great lengths to look just right, and you need to be aware of a new hairstyle or a new dress. Make sure to compliment her on her good qualities.

Take Her Places She Wants to Go

Ask her opinion on places to go and things to do. You may find she likes different things than you and they may be fun for you as well.

Open Doors for Her

There's no substitute for good manners, so carry heavy items, open doors, let her go first, speak first, and generally be first.

Bring Her Gifts

It's the little things that impress her: flowers, candy, cards, and stuffed animals are important items for winning with young women.

Talk About Her Interests

To be a good listener and conversationalist you must learn to talk in terms of your date and her interests. I laugh when I recall the story of the man who talked about himself endlessly to his date, telling her all he had achieved. Finally he stopped and said, "Well, I've talked enough about myself. Let's talk about you for a while. What do *you* think about all I've accomplished?"

Listen to Her

Nothing will impress her more than listening attentively to what she's saying. Effective listening is a rare and valuable virtue.

Favorable Behavior for Young Women

Be On Time

I list this first because it will make you a standout. Running late is one of men's biggest frustrations with women. You can truly set yourself apart by forming the habit of being on time. Many women accept tardiness as a given and run late their entire lives. If you learn to *allow enough time,* you can be on time. Get in the habit of being ready a half-hour early, which will both lower your stress level and give you room in case things don't go exactly according to plan. What could be better than having a little extra time to sit and think a few minutes before you go? Acquire this habit and you'll be rare and revered by men and women alike.

Learn About His Interests

It's important to learn something about his interests. I'll use sports as an example, since it's an interest to most guys. You'll be a hit with him when you know something about his favorite sport. If you know what's going on with his favorite team he'll be impressed. If you know when a sport he likes is on TV, or want to attend a game with him, you'll be a star. Get into the game with your guy; you'll find it can be fun, and will help you have a relationship that other girls envy.

Tell Him What You Like About Him

Men spend most of their lives seeking the approval of their significant other. Nothing does more to harm a relationship than disapproval. Be quick to tell him if you like his smile, his car, the way he dresses, or the way he treats you. Praise the things you like about him and he'll go to any length to do more of them.

Smile A Lot

Most young women already know this, but if you don't you're missing a huge opportunity. A nice smile from anyone on Earth feels great. We need those smiles to know we're doing all right. The expression you wear on your face is much more important than the clothes you wear on your back. A smile is an inexpensive way to improve your looks.

Stay Positive

Find the good and praise it. Learn to look for what's right, instead of what's wrong. Believe good will happen, learn to look on the bright side of things, and be sure to count your blessings. Avoid gossip; it lowers your self-esteem and makes you look bad. It's not easy to stay clear of gossip, but when you do, you put yourself in a different league. When you're tempted to criticize, bite on your tongue.

Make Him Feel Special

The best way to make him feel special is by showing approval. Let him know the things he does that you approve, like being a safe driver, taking you places where you feel comfortable, and not pushing you to do things you don't want to do. Another important way to make him feel special is to focus your attention on him and never flirt with other guys when he's with you. If you sit close to him or take his hand, you can be sure you're scoring points.

Keep Your Dignity

Stand firm on things that are truly important to you. Don't let him or anyone else push you to go against your inner voice. By all means don't be "easy." No young man respects or wants to be with an easy girl. It might appear that they do at first, but it's only to satisfy their carnal desires and then you'll be out. Young men want a girl they're proud to be with, and who has the respect of others. Go slowly with all aspects of your relationship, and make each phase special. Expect him to treat you like a lady and accept no less. There's nothing wrong with refusing his advances unless they're right for you. In all areas of life it's important to learn to decline gracefully. It's usually not the refusal that upsets people, but the way it's done. Learn to say, "Not right now" or "Not yet." Tell him you understand his feelings, but need more time. Say, "I'm flattered by your affection, but have pictured this happening in a different way." These attitudes will make him respect and want you all the more.

Unfavorable Behavior for Young Men

Not Treating Her Specially
If you don't treat her special you'll lose her respect and that of her friends. You're better off without a date than one you're not excited about.

Foul Language or Crude Remarks
It's not cool to use bad language or be crude and it's unacceptable on a date. Be strong enough to avoid this pitfall.

Pushing Her to Do Things She Doesn't Want to Do
Let her show you what she does and doesn't want to do. Look for her clues and act accordingly.

Thinking of Her as an Object
A young woman should not be thought of as an item. Think of her as the sensitive human being she really is and learn to appreciate her character. Don't focus too much on how she looks and what might be in it for you. It's natural and healthy to admire a pretty girl, but don't become obsessed with the physical side; you'll make bad decisions if you're led by this alone.

Being Rough or Aggressive with Her
Save the rough treatment for the locker room. Young women don't like to be shoved, pushed, or hit. Treat her gently and with care. Guys can be rough without realizing it; your aggressiveness is better suited to the football field.

Smoking

There's not one good thing about smoking. You're hurting yourself and your chances with the girls if you smoke. I wouldn't consider going out with a young woman who smoked, and many young women feel the same about guys. Where people are smoking, they foul the air and make everyone's clothing stink. Finally, and most importantly, smoking will kill you. There are over 200,000 cases of lung cancer in our country each year, and 87 percent of them are smokers.

Focusing on Yourself

If you want to succeed with a young woman, keep the spotlight on her. Talk about things she wants to talk about, and ask her lots of questions about herself.

Unfavorable Behavior for Young Women

Talking too much

To succeed with guys, save some of your conversation for your girlfriends. Men generally prefer some quiet time along with the talk. Too much talking is just as bad as not enough.

Gossiping or Nagging

Gossip is never good unless it's good gossip, which is speaking about other people's virtues. Talk about what's right and overlook what's wrong. Instead of nagging, make requests, because men like to be dealt with directly. Men dislike reading between the lines, and they're not very good at it. Tell him what you want in plain, simple English.

Pouting or Complaining

No one enjoys being around someone that pouts or complains, so there's no place for either on a date. Put a smile on your face and keep it there. If something's not going the way you want, talk about it, change it, or live with it, but don't frown or grumble about it.

Blaming Him for what's Wrong
By accepting self-responsibility you eliminate blame. There's no place for blame in our lives. If you don't like something, change it, but don't blame. Remember: *If it's to be, it's up to me.*

Making Him Wait
Make a pact with yourself that you won't make him wait. To be on time is common decency and respect. If you're even five minutes late, apologize.

The following happened to me when I was sixteen. It concerns dating, and it's something all young people must learn. I'd just bought my first car, and my girlfriend Leslie and I went out for a drive. I paid too much attention to her and not enough to my driving. We were holding hands, talking, and occasionally kissing. After one of those quick kisses, I looked up and all the cars in front of me had come to a stop. I had only a second to make one of three choices: I could hit the car in front of me, drive into a ditch off to the right, or pull out into the left lane. I chose the left lane, which was the wrong choice. An approaching car hit us head-on, even though we had come to a complete stop.

The accident was serious enough to cost our insurance company sixteen thousand dollars back in 1959. I had no car for the rest of my high-school years. The consequences of an auto accident can ruin or cost you your life. *When driving, never take your eyes off the road.* Most accidents occur when people are changing a radio station, putting in a tape or CD, trying to read a map, or just not paying attention for a second or two. Please think about this and take me literally.

The Boy / Girl Theory

I'm ending this section with what I call "the Boy/Girl Theory." It applies to friendship, dating, and negotiating business deals. The theory is about learning patience and resisting the desire for instant gratification. In other words, learning not to play your cards too fast. The boy/girl theory is especially applicable to the "now generation." Many young people today haven't learned the value of patience; therefore, when they have a desire, they want it satisfied instantly. Seeking immediate gratification won't serve you well in dating or in life. Most of the best things in life take time. It's good to remind yourself that *Nature never acts in haste, and since we are part of nature, neither should we.*

Consider the way you deal with someone you're dating. When you first begin, it's not uncommon to want to be with him or her every minute. If you want to keep their attention and build a lasting relationship, it will benefit you to apply the boy/girl theory. That means not being available all the time. Too big a dose of anything—or anyone—detracts from the richness and pleasure that come from moderation. When you're not always available, it shows the other person that you have a life other than them and makes them appreciate you more. It's common knowledge that we want the things we can't readily have, and often take for granted what we can have at will. A healthy relationship requires that you have a variety of interests, and you'll be better off occasionally doing things with members of your own gender, instead of going out every day with your boyfriend or girlfriend. By having other interests and not being available every minute, you'll be a more rounded and interesting individual, and the time you spend with the one you're dating will be more special for both of you.

The same is true about talking on the phone, holding hands, and kissing. All of those are wonderful in moderation, but you lose some of their beauty and meaning by doing them all the time. Being a little unpredictable and independent is a good thing. Not getting everything you want exactly when you want it is a good thing too. Anticipation is a big part of the excitement of life. Don't call him or her every day, and don't go out together every night. Be thoughtful, kind, and considerate, but not available every second. This will enrich your relationship.

The essence of the boy/girl theory is that people want what they can't have easily. Someone who's easy is often taken for granted and not shown proper respect or appreciation. In relationships, being a little hard-to-get, a little aloof, and somewhat unpredictable, is a good thing. I don't mean playing mind games, just being sensible. Don't you appreciate food, water, and sleep more after going without them for a while? If you want the best relationship you can have, remember the boy/girl theory.

School

Now that you've had at least ten years of school, it's a good time to take a look and see if you're on the right track. If you keep doing what you've been doing, will it get you where you want to go? If you know you're on the right track, keep doing what you've been doing. If you don't feel you're on track, it's time to change your actions.

School isn't as much about grades as you might think. It's much more about what you actually learn while getting your grades. You have the opportunity to *learn* a great deal, and that should be your goal. It's important to your future that your grades be an accurate reflection of your learning. As an employer for twenty-five years, I was never once concerned about what grades people earned in school. What I cared about was the kind of people they were, their habits and attitudes, and the depth of their technical knowledge. The point is to really learn and not to think only of your grades.

If I'd Known Then What I Know Now

This is not only the time to learn English, math, and history, but also the time to perfect your social skills and get involved in sports, drama, music, and other school activities. Work on your ability to get along with others every day. Pay no attention to any bad things people say about you; simply live so no one will believe them. Many young people are too concerned about what others think of them. Be sure to live in a way that you are happy with yourself. It's only those who are happy with themselves who can give to others. If you're doing the right things, don't worry about what others might think. Your fellow students have their own agendas and may not be looking out for you. Henry David Thoreau gave us some good advice when he said, "Learn to march to the beat of your own drum." He was an individualist who was unconcerned with popular opinion—and better off for it!

Your school years are a preview of how you'll behave later in life. The habits you form in school are the ones you'll take into your business and personal life. If you study hard in school, you'll likely work hard. If you cheat in school, you'll likely cheat in business or other endeavors.

One of the best habits you can form is the habit of *action*. Do today what needs to be done. It's a very bad habit to put things off. One of the signs of success is to do a job as soon as you get it. This is the habit known as *"Act now."* Only action will bring you success. It doesn't matter how smart you are if you're not in action.

Everyone's success depends on his or her ability to get along well with people. Learn to get along with all your teachers. This will save you much misery, and will teach you to get along with all types of people. A key to getting along well with others is learning to speak other people's virtues—say positive things about them and keep any negative thoughts to yourself. Many young people spend too much time gossiping. If you must gossip, learn to be known for good gossip. It's natural that others won't think or behave exactly as you want them to. It's a major move to learn to *live and let live.* Criticizing others serves no useful purpose, and it makes you look bad. You'll be a standout if you eliminate criticism and negative gossip and practice praise. You'll also feel better about yourself.

Career

Very few people know early in their lives what they want to do as a profession. This decision is second only to marriage in terms of its importance, and shouldn't be left to chance. *When thinking about a career, the first thing to ask yourself is, What am I passionate about?* The most rewarding career will be the one you wake up every day excited to pursue. A person who does something just for the money or prestige rarely does as good a job or enjoys his work as much as those who follow their passions. Be sure to pursue your dreams. Whatever career you choose, there's a reason why successful people are successful: *Successful people are successful because they're willing to do the things unsuccessful people are unwilling to do.* Those things include:

♦ Always being on time

♦ Exceeding expectations

♦ Thinking of others welfare as well as their own

♦ Staying late or coming in early when necessary

♦ Maintaining a positive attitude and cheerful disposition

♦ Making people feel important

♦ Keeping their work areas neat and clean

♦ Doing a job as soon as they get it

♦ Paying attention to detail by being meticulous in all they do

The compensation you receive in business is directly related to how easily you can be replaced. The harder you are to replace, the more valuable you are. Think of the difference between a minimum-wage job and being a neurosurgeon. It's obvious that one is much more easily replaced than the other, and there's no comparison in pay. Consider this when you make a career decision. Remember the saying "Slow and steady wins the race." Life is a marathon, not a sprint. If you can pick the right career early and stay with it, you'll have the opportunity to become one of the most knowledgeable people in your chosen field. That will make you hard to replace, and thus very valuable. Life is full of change, and you must learn to embrace change, but marriage and career are two areas in which it will serve you best to get it right the first time.

Finance

According to one of my mentors, *"Economics comes after breathing."* There's no question that economics are extremely important. It's a good feeling when you can afford the things you need and want. I still remember looking forward to the day that I could walk into a store and pay cash for the clothes I wanted. My next goal was to pay cash for a car, and finally, to pay cash for my house. It's wise to avoid debt as much as possible. Being in debt is like having a wolf biting at your heels. Don't even consider credit-card debt, as it's outrageous. If you use a credit card, be sure you pay it off in full every month from the start. You might be forced to take on some debt at first, but my advice is to become a bit fanatical about getting rid of it as soon as possible.

The process of financial success begins with a systematic savings program and learning to live well within your means. As you get older and more successful, you'll need a secondary source of income. I'll cover that in detail in a later lesson. Your initial job is to learn to save and to limit your wants. One philosopher put it this way: "To be a financial success, you must harness the wild steed of desire." As a rule, save a minimum of 10 percent of everything you earn. If you start your savings program at age sixteen, you'll be amazed at how much money you'll have saved by the time you're twenty-five. *It's not how much you make, it's how much you keep.* There are people who make a lot of money, but keep very little. Many don't have peace of mind because they think only of spending. On the other hand, we've all heard of the proverbial minimum-wage worker who didn't earn much, but had a good savings program, no debt, a life full of happiness, and money left at the end. One thing to learn early about finance is that no matter how well you're doing, rainy days will come and you must be prepared for them. The most important thing to remember about finance is: *If you want to become wealthy, you must think of saving as well as getting.*

Health

Health is too vast and complicated a subject to cover in depth here. My objective is to touch on some of the health risks we all face, many of which are preventable by intelligent action.

At your age, you might feel that health is of little concern, but good health is a must for success and happiness. You're probably strong and healthy now, but might not know that the habits you form now will affect your future health. As you get older, you'll think more about your health, and in your later years it will become a prime concern. The way you live now will have great impact on how you fare later. Only the wisest among you will heed this advice, but those who do will benefit greatly.

Two primary keys to good health are diet and exercise. Most

young people are active, but diet is often another story. The crucial key to giving yourself the best chance for good health is to *eat lots of fruits and vegetables, only small amounts of meat, stay away from sugar, eat a balanced diet, and drink lots of good water.* That's it in a nutshell. You can read books on diet that will go into great detail and be helpful, but it all boils down to the above. If you're interested in learning more about diet, read *Renewal* by Timothy J. Smith, M.D. He offers valuable information for those of you who want to give yourself the best chance for a longer life.

The only word I can think of for smoking is *stupid.* Nothing good can be said about smoking. It can ruin your health and kill you. It's addictive, offensive, and can have a negative impact on your relationships with others. Smoking stinks, is very expensive, causes people to avoid you, and offers no benefits. Please avoid it at all costs—don't even try it.

Skin cancer is affecting as many people now as all other cancers combined; 10,000 people die from it annually. More people between thirteen and twenty-five are showing up with the disease. Glenn Parker, a former football player for the New York Giants, admitted to being a beach bum who loved to spend time in the sun. He had surgery to remove from his leg a three-inch-square tumor caused by skin cancer. Severe sunburns as a child can lead to cancer in later life. Wear sunglasses and a hat, use sunscreen, and avoid the sun in the hottest part of the day—noon until three.

Your Thoughts

Much of my thinking on this subject has come from the books *Think and Grow Rich,* by Napoleon Hill, and *As a Man Thinketh,* by James Allen. Most people haven't been taught the importance of their thoughts. It's imperative for you to learn that *Thoughts are things.* How your life turns out will depend on your thoughts. *You're precisely where you are today because of your previous thinking, and your current thoughts are a preview of your life's coming attractions.* You'll succeed or fail based on your thinking. When you get control of your thoughts, you can take control of your future, and enter a far different world than most of those around you.

Do you realize that you can literally *think and grow rich?* All achievements originate in thoughts. The first step to success is to define in writing exactly what you want, when you want it by, and what you're willing to give in return for it. Once you do this, read it daily and picture yourself already in possession of whatever it is you desire. As Napoleon Hill points out in his great book, *Think and Grow Rich, "The first step to riches is desire."* When I speak of desire here, I'm not talking about a wish, which is a desire to attain with no effort. I'm talking about a white-hot burning desire, an obsession with a goal that nothing can stop you from achieving.

Perhaps the most common cause of failure is the habit of quitting in the face of temporary defeat. In *Think and Grow Rich,* Hill tells the story of a miner obsessed with finding gold. He dug and searched for many years, and finally threw up his hands in defeat, selling his mine to the first person that made him an offer. The man who bought the mine dug only three feet before hitting the largest gold vein in Nevada history, the Comstock Lode. Many successful people say that their greatest success came just beyond the point where defeat had overtaken them. It truly is darkest just before the dawn. You're only defeated when you quit, and if you want something badly enough, you won't quit. It's comforting to remember that each failure carries with it the seed of a greater triumph. Most people who succeed live through rough startup periods, get bad breaks, and have to go through many heartbreaking struggles before achieving their goals.

If I'd Known Then What I Know Now

You must develop the quality of faith if you're going to succeed. When you have ideas that you feel strongly about and truly believe in, you put in motion the factors that will make them come true. Thoughts given strong feeling, mixed with faith, immediately begin transforming themselves into reality. What you think and then feel strongly about will begin to happen. Our minds take on the nature of the influences that dominate them. You can develop faith by repeating affirmative orders to your mind. By telling yourself over and over the things you want to be true, your mind finally accepts them and they happen. That's why it's so very important to never say anything about yourself that you don't *want* to be true.

Here are some characteristics that lead to success:

♦ Doing more than you're paid to do

♦ Having definite written goals

♦ Developing a vivid imagination

♦ Enthusiasm

♦ Self-control

♦ Persistence and determination

♦ Tolerance

♦ Initiative

♦ A pleasing personality

♦ Decisiveness—reaching decisions quickly and changing them slowly

To succeed, one of the first qualities to cultivate is a pleasing personality. It's critical that you be able to attract the right people into your life. *People take on the nature, habits, and power of thought of those they associate with.* To succeed, you will want to surround yourself with a group of people who share your goals and dreams. One of the most common weaknesses people have is the habit of leaving their minds open to the negative influences of others.

In summary, you'll only succeed in life if you learn to control your thoughts. Your mind is like a garden, and your thoughts are what you allow to grow in it. You must eliminate the negative thinking, or weeds, and only allow positive thinking, or good seeds, to grow if you want to succeed. Your mottoes will become:

In with the positive and out with the negative;

In with the good and out with the bad;

In with love and out with hate;

In with truth and out with lies;

In with praise and out with criticism;

In with courage and out with fear;

In with generosity and out with greed;

In with action and out with laziness;

In with good habits and out with bad.

Your mind can't focus on positive and negative thoughts at the same time, so the secret is to keep your mind full of positive thoughts.

Habits

A habit is a constant, often unconscious inclination to perform an act, acquired through its frequent repetition. You see it when a baby sucks his thumb, when you have a cup of coffee at the same time every day or when you bite your nails. All habits are formed through repetition. After enough repetition an act becomes a habit and you become its slave. *The biggest difference between those who succeed and those who fail generally lies in the difference of their habits.* It's important to form good habits. When an act is repeated over and over, it becomes easy, and when it becomes easy, it's our nature to perform it often. The way to acquire good habits is to identify the ones you want and repeat them often. Once you have acquired the right habits your future is almost guaranteed. The following "Good Habits" are among the ones Og Mandino talks about in his fine book, *The Greatest Salesman in the World.*

Start each day with love in your heart. This is the most important habit you can acquire. Love can open people's hearts, and no one can defend against it. Your first good habit is to learn to look upon all things with love.

A woman saw three white-bearded old men sitting in her yard. Thinking they might be hungry, she invited them in. Since her husband wasn't there they refused her offer. When he came home she invited them in again. They explained to her that they never enter a house together. One said his name was Wealth; his two friends were Success and Love. He asked which of them she wanted to ask in. Her husband suggested they invite Wealth and thus fill their home with riches. The wife wanted to invite Success. Their daughter-in-law, who was listening, asked, "Would it not be better to invite Love, so you can fill your home with love?" Heeding her advice, the couple invited Love to be their guest. Love arose and started toward the house, and the other two also got up, and followed him. The woman was surprised, since they had only invited Love. The old men explained that Love does not follow Wealth or Success, but where there is Love, Wealth and Success can follow. Wealth and Success are also empty without Love.

Persist until you succeed. Everyone fails from time to time, but you're not defeated until you quit. Get in the habit of finishing what you start. If you persist you will succeed. You can't succeed if you quit or run at the first sign of trouble; therefore, you must learn to persevere if you want to succeed. Each misfortune carries within it the seed of a future success. Nothing worthwhile comes easily, and you never know where success will be hiding. If you don't succeed at first, take another step, and if it fails, another. Never forget, *Small attempts repeated will complete any undertaking.*

Display your uniqueness and hide your similarities. Each person is different from all others and you shouldn't try to be like anyone else. No one else can do exactly what you can, and no one else will ever be just like you. It's important for you to be who you really are and not imitate others. Put your uniqueness on display and take pride in your differences.

Live each day as if it were your last. The truth is, we don't know when our last day will be. By following this advice you take time to do the things that are most important. You call the people you care about, enjoy each event or encounter, and stay in the moment. Since there's nothing you can do about yesterday or tomorrow, it's wise to make the most of the present. Why worry about what happened in the past or might happen in the future? Most things you worry about never happen anyway. It's good advice to not put off until tomorrow what you can do today. By forming the habit of living each day as if it were your last, you eliminate most doubt, worry, and procrastination. What dying person wouldn't give all they have for a little more time?

Become the master of your emotions. Each of these habits is important, but this one seems to be difficult for many people to acquire. Learning to control your emotions is crucial to success and happiness. When you find yourself yelling, pouting, fighting, arguing, and generally upset, you're not controlling your emotions. Studying the natural world, we see that all Nature is a cyclical process. The tides advance and recede, winter comes and goes, flowers bloom and fade. Since we are part of Nature, our moods also rise and fall. When we wake up each day, we don't know what our mood will be. One day we're happy and the next we are sad. We have the capacity to recognize and control our moods. We can learn to understand that today's sadness will turn into tomorrow's joy. We can make allowances for those who are in a bad mood today, for we know that tomorrow they will be a joy to approach. By mastering your moods you master your destiny.

Laugh at the world. Laughing is one of the secrets to a long life. People are most comical when they take themselves too seriously. Laughter reduces things to their proper size. As long as you look up to others you won't become arrogant. It's only with laughter and happiness that we can really be successful.

Multiply your value. To multiply your value, you must set lofty goals, and can never be content with your performance of today. If a tiny seed can become a mighty oak, think what you can become. You can multiply your value by helping others, because they in turn can teach others what you've taught them, and the learning can continue throughout time.

Act now. Your dreams, goals, and plans are of no value unless you follow them with action. With action you won't put off until tomorrow what you can do today. When you face temptation you'll act to remove yourself from it, and when you're tempted to quit you'll take action and more action until you complete your task. No map can take you one step of your journey unless you act. Only action will determine your value.

These habits can take you to the top, and the best way to learn them is to pick up *The Greatest Salesman in the World,* by Og Mandino, and literally follow his instructions. In nine months you can acquire all the habits we've discussed. The paperback version of the book sells for less than ten dollars.

The Lesson in a Nutshell

♦ You set the stage for the balance of your life by the habits you form during ages sixteen to twenty-five.

♦ It's time for you to accept full responsibility for what happens in your life.

♦ You make a good impression by showing other people you're impressed with them.

♦ Don't be so sure you're right when dealing with more experienced people.

♦ Good advice isn't always peaches and cream—that's why so few follow it.

♦ He's not a friend who always makes you laugh, but he who sometimes makes you cry.

♦ It's best to avoid arguing with your parents.

♦ It's time to eliminate blame from your life. By eliminating blame you eliminate anger, as almost all anger distills down to blame.

♦ Form the habit of looking for what's right instead of what's wrong.

♦ Successful people are successful because they're willing to do the things unsuccessful people are unwilling to do.

♦ Whom you marry may be the most important decision of your life.

♦ The best marriage is based on being best friends above all else.

♦ Trying to change other people is a waste of time. Live and let live.

♦ Don't expect other people to be like you.

♦ Eliminate criticism.

♦ Make your career decision based on your *passion.*

♦ Your worth in business depends on how easily you can be replaced.

♦ Life is a marathon, not a sprint.

♦ Change is inevitable — so embrace it.

♦ The habit of saving is a must for achieving financial freedom.

♦ Good health depends on exercising, drinking lots of water, and eating lots of fruits and vegetables.

♦ How your life turns out depends on your thoughts.

♦ The first step to riches is a burning desire.

♦ Never say anything about yourself that you don't *want* to be true.

♦ Success depends on forming good habits and becoming their slave.

A Few Profound Thoughts

♦ Love is without question life's greatest experience.

♦ All I give is given to myself.

♦ An old young man will be a young old man.

♦ Failure is a pre-requisite to success.

♦ Make your word your bond—even if it costs you your last dime.

♦ Don't compare yourself to others; there will always be those who are greater and lesser than you.

♦ Small attempts repeated will complete any undertaking.

♦ Begin with the end in mind.

♦ If you always do what you say you're going to do, I can build an empire around you. If you sometimes do what you say you're going to do, you're just another headache for me.

♦ The faintest ink is stronger than the strongest memory.

♦ Avoid every form of excess.

♦ The essence of life is making and keeping promises.

♦ Great estates may venture more, but little ships should stay near shore (learn your boundaries).

♦ You can make more friends in two months by becoming genuinely interested in them than you can in two years trying to get them interested in you.

♦ Only inexperience makes a young man do what an old man says is impossible.

♦ There is no right way to do the wrong thing.

Lesson Three

Ages 26 – 40

Family, Marriage, Parenting, Others, Career, Finance, Health, Your Thoughts, The Lesson in a Nutshell, A Few Profound Thoughts.

Overview

Each phase of life has its pluses and minuses, and I'm happy to report that each stage of my life has been better than the one before it. I'm certain that each would have been even better had I known then what I know now. Think of this period as the "foundation stage" of adulthood. Your energy level and reflexes are usually at their best during these years. It's easier to recover from mistakes made early in life than the ones you make as you get older. Life is a little like a basketball game, in the sense that once the game begins, your ability to recover from problems decreases as the clock runs down. If you're down twenty points at the end of the first quarter, it's not nearly as big a deal as if it's the last five minutes. The same is true of life. The wise person gets more serious about his or her future from this point onward. It's time to set your sights high, as it's no more work to aim high than to aim low.

Your career will become especially important during these years. Some think they can outsmart their competitors, and maybe they can, but all things being even remotely equal, the ones who out-work the rest and have the best human-relations skills will get the big prize. *All things being equal, people do business with people they like, and all things being unequal, people still do business with people they like, if at all possible.* People will go to great lengths to do business with people they like, and if it means they have to pay a slightly higher price or allow more time to get something they want, they'll do it to work with someone they like.

These are the years when you might get married and start a family, buy your first house, and probably meet some of the friends who will be with you for life. Nurture those friendships and the rewards will be great. Among the rewards of close friendships are the memories you'll share and enjoy over the years. These are the people who'll remember and understand many of your life's victories and defeats. Consider becoming active in your community through church, clubs, or civic organizations. You'll be rewarded for giving back to your community. Remember: *All I give is given to myself.*

During these years, you should experience great personal growth, and the easiest way to grow is by surrounding yourself with people who are smarter than you are.

Some Keys to a Happy Life

♦ Compliment someone every day.

♦ Watch a sunrise or sunset.

♦ Live beneath your means.

♦ Treat others the way they want to be treated.

♦ Forget about trying to keep up with the Joneses.

♦ Remember people's names.

♦ Pray for wisdom and courage instead of for things.

♦ Be tough-minded and tenderhearted.

♦ Be kinder than you have to be.

♦ Satisfy people's greatest emotional need—the need to feel important.

♦ Keep your promises.

♦ Learn to show cheerfulness—even when you don't feel it.

♦ Remember that overnight success usually takes about fifteen years.

♦ Leave everything better than you found it.

♦ Remember that winners do the things that losers are unwilling to do.

♦ Don't rain on other people's parades.

♦ Don't waste an opportunity to tell someone you love, "I love you."

Family

To say that family is important in every stage of life seems obvious; however, many people don't live in a way that reflects that knowledge. Given another chance, I'd think more about family and act accordingly. I'd call and visit my parents and relatives more often. I'd be better at remembering their special days, and more appreciative of their raising me. I'd do more listening, and spend more time with my family while they were young. I'd avoid having my children participate in too many events, and let them choose the events they want to do most, so neither they nor I would be driven crazy by too hectic a schedule. I'd restore the tradition of the entire family sitting down at the table together for dinner. It's a special setting where members can share stories of their day and their lives. We only get one chance, and these are the people who really count. Friends come and go throughout our lives, but our family is usually there from start to finish.

Because of their sensitivities and compassion, women seem to have a better handle on family than men. Your spouse's family is usually very important to him or her, so it's important to accept and embrace your in-laws to help build family unity. Many young people take their families for granted, and by the time they realize how important relatives are, it's often too late.

If you don't have good family traditions, be the one to start them. For the past decade our family has spent Thanksgiving together, and it's become the most special time of the year for us. My wife and I recently became partners with my brother Paul on thirty-five acres in Whitefish, Montana. We just finished building the house, and plan for it to be in our family for generations. We want the ranch to be a place where relatives and friends can enjoy winter and summer sports and get to know each other in a special setting. We want to pass it down from generation to generation.

Marriage

If you marry, it will probably be the most important decision you'll ever make. The relationship between husband and wife has significant direct effect on each partner's every day. If there isn't peace between them, there's rarely any peace for either. Each partner's mood greatly affects the other. *In the best marriages, the partners are truly best friends.* You're on sound footing when your love for each other exceeds your need for each other.

In good marriages both spouses are supportive and look out for one another's welfare. Both are kind, polite, and anxious to help each other. In a healthy marriage, there's little criticism and lots of praise. Generally speaking, a man's happy if his wife's happy. He takes it personally if she's not, and feels a responsibility to help her. If her mood's not good, or if she's worried in any way, it affects him until she's at peace again.

In an earlier lesson, we discussed the importance of first impressions. The same can be said of new beginnings. It's advisable to get off on the right foot to help a relationship become a good and lasting one. Young people are often too focused on themselves, and this prevents them from forming the best relationship from the start. Being self-centered when you're young is normal; it's less a fault than an issue of maturity. You can learn to focus on others by maturing, or take the word of someone who's traveled the road before you. If you're willing to learn from someone who's been there, you can save yourself a lot of pain. To get a good start in a relationship, put plenty of attention on your mate's needs and desires from the beginning.

Marriage is very different now from when I got married. In most cases today, both spouses work, which makes it important for both to help run the home. Household chores like making the bed, cooking, washing dishes, cleaning, and doing laundry fall more on both, since both are providers. At nineteen, I was much too young to get married and took too much for granted. My attitude was that I was the provider and my wife should manage all the other aspects of our home. I feel very foolish and ashamed as I look back on those days. If I'd known then what I know now, I'd have understood that a healthy marriage is a fully integrated partnership. I know now that marriage is about being in tune with each other's needs on a daily basis, and having a caring attitude. Having a total attitude of care for your spouse will make each of you feel respected and acknowledged.

If I'd known then what I know now, I'd have been more attentive, understanding that anything to do with the home is also my responsibility. It would have been easy for me to encourage my wife, and do some special things for her each day, to show her how much I cared and how important she was to the health of our family.

Here's a list of some things you need to know about men and women in order to build good and lasting relationships.

Realize that your spouse won't behave as you do. Men and women are very different in how they react to situations. Men are problem solvers who go into that mode given any opportunity. Women like to share information and air their feelings. Often, a woman simply wants to be heard, without getting any advice. A man immediately starts offering solutions and advice, and that can cause friction. When my wife tells me something that sounds like a problem, I ask her, "Is this something you want me to just listen to, or are you looking for a solution?" It's critical that each of the partners respect and accept their differences. *Live and let live* applies in spades to marriage.

Learn not to offer unsolicited advice. Men feel they can solve their own problems and will go to great lengths to do so. Asking for advice is usually a last resort. Most men feel they got quite enough advice growing up, and the last thing they want is mothering. Examples of this are, "Why don't you park over there?" "You're driving too fast," "You're following too close," and "Don't keep the refrigerator door open so long." It's not that these aren't valid points, but they'll surely lead to trouble and hard feelings. Men often offer unsolicited advice as well, and it's equally troubling to their wives.

Don't give any more detail than is needed. Generally, women want details and men just want facts. This can be very frustrating no matter who's telling the story. To get along peacefully, he must learn to listen to more detail than he wants, and she must be willing to accept less detail than she prefers. By *detail* I mean things like her asking him to go to the store for her. All he wants to know is what she wants him to get, but she'll often want to tell him what store to go to, where in the store the item is located, and how much he should pay for it. If she's had a dream, she wants to tell him all the details, but all he wants to know is what the essence of it was.

Men need to learn more empathy. By *empathy* I mean understanding your wife's world. Respect the number of things she's dealing with each day. She's taking care of most household chores, and the children, and she's usually the one covering family birthdays and other important events, like Thanksgiving and Christmas. There's an endless list of tasks that she does, while you often focus exclusively on your work and sports. It shouldn't be surprising if it takes her twice as long as you do to get ready to go somewhere, so just be patient.

Men tend to take things literally. When she makes a statement like "You never take me out anymore," he might respond, "What are you talking about? We just went out last week." What she meant was, "I'd like to go out now." When she uses words like *always, never, every,* and *none,* she doesn't necessarily mean them literally. Men are quick to defend against these words. She's sure he doesn't listen to her, and he's sure he *is* listening, because he can repeat what she said, even though he often doesn't understand what she means. The only sure way to know how your spouse feels about anything is to ask.

A mistake both spouses make repeatedly is offering the method of caring they prefer, instead of the one their partner prefers. A man probably won't care about getting a birthday card, so he fails to get his wife one. She wanted one, and feels he doesn't care about her needs. She may want to talk to her mother each week, and therefore bugs him to call his. She may want to talk about her hair, dress, and the way the table needs to be set, while he wants to talk about the stock market, sports, and what's for dinner. We can get along well once we start to think about our partners in terms of how *they* want to be treated instead of how *we* want to be treated. Most of us were taught "Do unto others as you would have them do unto you." A much better approach is "Do unto others as *they* would have you do unto them."

Parenting

Given the importance of this responsibility, it's a subject about which the majority of people don't know as much as they need to. This is the area of my life where I'd like to have a "do-over" more than in any other. Parenting comes at a time when we're still quite young and have many other things going on in our lives. As I sit here with time to reflect, parenting looks much different than it did when my daughter, Shirley, was born. At nineteen I was still an adolescent and clueless about the meaning of being a parent. The young people of today seem to be better educated on parenting than my generation was. The "Information Revolution" has made much more knowledge available. Parenting is a huge responsibility, and the first step is having a strong desire to be a good parent, and learning all you can on the subject. There's hardly a more precious picture than a man and woman working together to raise their children properly.

If I'd known then what I know now, I'd have realized that the first seven years are the most formative of a child's life. Many of the habits and values they'll have forever are established during this time. I'd have understood that a child's feelings are more sensitive than an adult's. When we scold or spank a child, it's a major event in their tender little worlds.

We can learn from our children: A man became angry with his three-year-old daughter when she "wasted" a roll of gold wrapping paper decorating a box to put under their Christmas tree.

The next morning, the little girl brought the gift to her father and said, "This is for you, Daddy." He was embarrassed by his earlier overreaction, but his anger flared again when he found that the box was empty. He yelled at her, "Don't you know that when you give someone a present, there's supposed to be something inside it?" The little girl looked up at him tearfully and said, "Oh, Daddy, it's not empty. I blew kisses into the box, all for you." Crushed, the father put his arms around his little girl and begged her forgiveness. He kept that gold box by his bed for years. Whenever he felt discouraged, he would take out an imaginary kiss and remember the love of the child who put it there.

Children need to know they're special, precious little beings who are loved. I'm encouraged today by how many fathers spend ample time with their children. Looking back, I hardly knew my own father. He was a navy man and was gone a great deal of time. In the navy life, it was common for the mother to raise the children and deal with the majority of problems. I didn't spend enough time with my children, and it's one of my biggest regrets. In the last ten years I've built a much better relationship with them, but if I'd known then what I know now, I'd have taken my role much more seriously and done all the fatherly things I should have, and wish I had, done.

I'd have held them and talked to them more as infants, and treated them as if they understood it all. I'd have listened to their innocent explanations and tried much harder to grasp what was going on in their world. I'd have been more a part of their birthday parties, and would have spent much more one-on-one time with them. I'd have taken them to places they wanted to go, and made sure we had an annual vacation. I'd have taken them to see more movies and then discussed with them what we'd seen and how they felt about it. I'd have gone to their PTA meetings, and talked with their teachers about their progress and about how each teacher saw them as students and as people. Evening meals together would have been a must, and I'd have been more careful about just what kind of example I was setting for them. I'd have done less correcting and more connecting. You don't get a second chance on this one, so be sure to do it right the first time.

I'm fortunate that my children have been forgiving, and have given me the chance to be the kind of dad I wish I'd been earlier. I give my wife, Lisa, the credit for teaching me in this most important area of life. By example and coaching, she opened my eyes to the true importance of family. This is especially amazing since these weren't her children. With her help, I improved my relationships with my children and have become the dad I wanted to be.

How Much Are You Worth?

Late, tired, and irritated, a man came home from work to find his five-year-old son waiting for him at the door. The boy wanted to know how much money his dad made per hour. Wondering what made him ask such a thing, his father angrily told him it was none of his business. The little boy still wanted to know. The father finally told him it was twenty dollars an hour.

Head bowed, the little boy asked whether he could borrow

ten dollars. The father was furious, thinking the only reason the boy had asked how much money he made was so he could borrow some to buy a toy or some other nonsense. The father marched him straight to his room and put him to bed. He suggested the boy think about why he was being so selfish, and reminded him that he worked long, hard hours every day and had no time for such childish games.

After an hour, the man had calmed down, and began thinking he might have been a little hard on his son. Maybe there was something the boy really needed to buy, and he didn't ask for money very often. The man went to the door of his little boy's room and opened it.

He picked up his son and told him it had been a long day and he was sorry he had taken his aggravation out on him. He gave him the ten dollars. The little boy sat straight up, beaming. Then he reached under his pillow and pulled out some more crumpled bills. Seeing that the little boy already had some money, the father began to get angry again. The little boy slowly counted out his money, then looked up at his father, who wondered why the boy wanted more money if he already had some. The little one shared that he'd needed more because he hadn't had enough, but now he did. "I have twenty dollars now, Daddy. Can I buy an hour of your time?"

I recently read an interesting article on teen smoking and drinking. It said that parents who monitor the television their children watch and the music they listen to have far fewer problems with their children. Parents who set sensible rules reduce the risks of their children smoking, drinking, or using drugs. Some of those guidelines included turning off the TV during dinner, banning music with offensive lyrics, knowing where the children are after school, imposing curfews, assigning regular chores, and eating dinner together on a regular schedule.

Many parents today seem reluctant to discipline their children properly. No discipline says to the child that you don't care. Children need and crave discipline, because it tells them you love them and care enough to do the hard job of teaching them right from wrong.

Others

To truly understand the subject of others, let's begin with the rare and precious virtue of empathy. Empathy means having the ability to feel what others are feeling. Most people are focused on their own lives, working so hard to succeed that they don't take the time to put themselves in the place of others. We live in a society where everything seems to revolve around speed. Thinking about and caring for others requires that we slow down.

It's truly the rare person who understands the importance of *others* at an early age. Lacking empathy is often overlooked when you're young; as an adult, however, you become more accountable, and empathy becomes vital to your success. I'm defining success as achieving your goals in life, whatever they are. *The fastest way to achieve your goals is to help others achieve theirs.* By helping others succeed, you build a network of people who will help you. That network evolves as the people you help share with their friends and family what you did for them, thus spreading "good gossip" about you. You'll be surprised at the number of people who come to your rescue once you make it a habit to help others succeed. Help will come to you from places you can't even imagine.

Until you're on good terms with yourself, it's unlikely you'll be able to focus your attention on others. Only those who like themselves can be friendly and generous with others. How do you get on good terms with yourself? Why do so many people not like themselves? Shakespeare summed it up long ago in the admonition "This above all, to thine own self be true." We don't

If I'd Known Then What I Know Now

like ourselves when we do things we know we shouldn't do. Eating or drinking too much, not getting enough sleep, and speaking ill of others are examples, as are doing anything that hurts others, taking more than you give, not doing what you say you're going to do, and being disagreeable.

One of the first steps to good mental health is doing things that make you feel good about yourself. One thing that makes you feel best about yourself is giving to others. True giving is done without any thought of getting anything in return.

Generally, you succeed with others to the degree that you make them feel important. Everyone wants to feel important, to feel that they amount to something. There's a hunger for approval in all of us. By finding things you can approve in others, you help them like themselves better. The more they like themselves, the easier they are to get along with and the better for all. People act, or fail to act, largely to enhance their own egos. Through your use of courtesy you acknowledge the importance of others. The men and women who have the most influence on others are those who sincerely believe that people matter. People are *very* important to you and it's essential for you to develop this belief.

Here are some ways you can satisfy other people's need to feel important:

♦ Be on time. If you're even five minutes late, it tells others you had more important things to do.

♦ Send them thank-you notes. Be sure you thank people for the smallest things they do for you. It not only makes them feel important, but also encourages them to do more.

♦ Remember and use their names. People's names are very important to them, and they like hearing their names.

♦ Look people in the eyes.

♦ Talk about what *they* want to talk about.

♦ Ask their opinions.

♦ Compliment them whenever possible.

♦ Respond quickly to their requests.

♦ Be generous.

♦ Smile at them at every opportunity.

♦ Do promptly what you tell people you'll do.

How one chooses to live is a personal matter, and we shouldn't interfere uninvited. Learning to live and let live is a rare and wonderful virtue. To have peace and happiness, we must become tolerant of others, letting their perceived faults go unless they directly affect us. Benjamin Franklin said, "All my life I denied myself the pleasure of contradiction". You might think you're showing off your knowledge when you contradict people, but you're actually making them feel unimportant. Learn to put the spotlight on others and give them center stage. A common fault, and a sure way to lose with people, is trying to increase your own sense of importance by demeaning another. Negative talk and negative opinions give a bad impression. People judge you less by your opinion of yourself than by your opinion of others, and your opinion of other things, like your job and your competition. Learn to practice praise and eliminate criticism.

One sure-fire way to win with others is by learning to be a good listener. Listening is a rare and invaluable virtue. One of the highest compliments you can pay anyone is to truly listen. Most people prefer talking—generally about themselves. Effective listening is an art. Here are some proven ways to show people you're listening:

◆ Look directly at the person who's talking.

◆ Become deeply interested in what they're saying.

◆ Ask questions about what they're telling you.

◆ Never interrupt.

◆ Stick to *their* subject.

◆ Use their words to get your point across.

◆ Lean toward them while they're speaking.

People tend to act out their part in life according to the stage that's set for them. Let's say you're a fifth-grade teacher and want to leave the class for a few minutes. You say to Mary, "I've noticed all year how I can depend on you, Mary. You seem to always do the right thing. I know I can trust you to keep an eye on the class while I'm out, and that you'll tell me the truth about how things went when I return." By setting the stage for what you want Mary to do, you compel her to live up to your expectations. We all have a desire to do the appropriate thing. Knowing this, we can control a situation by setting the stage to get the result we want. If you want a meeting to be formal, set a formal stage; if you want it casual, set a casual stage. If you want it to be lighthearted, you start it with humor. Soon you'll begin setting the stage for your life in such a way that you continually get the result you want.

In dealing with others, we often see our own actions and attitudes reflected back to us as if we were looking into a mirror. If people aren't smiling at you, it's likely you're not smiling at them. If you're not receiving an attitude of care, it's likely you're not giving one. This is part of self-responsibility. We need to put our hand out if we want to get it shaken. If you're getting something you don't like from another, take a good look at what you've been giving them before making any negative judgment. To a large degree, you can control people's actions and attitudes by giving them what you want them to give you.

Not long ago, I was dealing with a person who usually showed up with a scowl and rarely smiled. It was upsetting to me and I found myself being drawn into her ways: I quit smiling and being friendly to her. This posture did nothing to remedy the situation or make me feel better, so I tried letting her see how good it felt to get smiles, and hugs, and a positive feeling each time she saw me, and over time this method worked. You need to give others whatever you want them to give you. It's much easier to get what you want from people by rewarding their good behavior than you could ever get by disapproving. If you want someone to smile more, you must show them how much you appreciate their smile. Compliment them on what a nice smile they have, tell them how it makes them look younger and happier and how good it feels to you. The only way to get people to do anything is to get them to want to do it.

Career

A career you enjoy and look forward to each day is a blessing. The best career is one you're truly excited about, one you enjoy reading and learning about, and one you feel makes a difference in society. By selecting the right career early and staying with it, you increase your chances of lifetime success immensely. Serious thought and research in the beginning pays big dividends later. Listen closely to your inner voice on this decision, and let your heart be involved. Before you decide on your career, look as far into your future as you can, and think carefully about exactly what and how you want your life to be twenty years from now.

Since commercial real estate was my business, I'll use it as an example of the kind of thinking it takes to make a good career decision. Once you decide on your chosen field, your next decision is what your specialty will be. In real estate, there's residential, commercial, and investment, to name a few. Each is unique, and requires different skills. Your choice of specialty can have great impact on your degree of success. You'll use the same thought process if your field is law, medicine, music, or any other.

If you chose residential real estate, you'd deal with emotional decision-makers and work nights and weekends. If you chose commercial real estate, your next decision would be which discipline to work in: choices include industrial, retail, office, research and development, or investment. Again, each of these is quite different and has it's own pluses and minuses. In commercial, you would deal more with logic than emotion, and you'd work normal business hours. A key decision is to decide where you want to work and live. You couldn't make a living doing commercial real estate in a small town, so you'd need to select a location with lots of potential, like Silicon Valley, Austin, Boston, Los Angeles, New York, Seattle, San Francisco, or Phoenix.

As you can see, each decision you make leads you to another and another. That's why you need to begin with the end in mind and work your way back to the present. Perhaps the most critical question to ask is "What do I really care about?" Are you willing to live anywhere to maximize your potential, or do you prefer to live where you are and get the best career you can in that location? If I'd known then what I know now, my first decision would be to pick a location I was wild about, a place I felt I would want to live the rest of my life. We live in Hawaii, which is often referred to as paradise, because the climate is perfect and there's lots of sunshine every day. If I'd known then what I know now I would seek and find a career right here.

Don't you think it makes sense to start your career in a place you love and plan to remain? Isn't it wonderful to be able to make these kinds of choices? Often, people don't realize they are the masters of their own destiny. You can live anywhere and become almost anything if you're willing to pay the price. Career is far too important a decision to leave to chance. In the real estate field, it's a disaster to try to change locations, as your knowledge of the people and properties is what determines most of your success. Think your career decision through carefully and make it turn out the way you want.

Once you make your career choice, it's important to view the company you work for as if it were your own. In reality, we're all in business for ourselves, no matter where we work. By thinking of the company as yours, you'll make better decisions.

♦ Always do what you say you're going to do.

♦ Be a little early for all commitments.

♦ Learn to under-commit and over-deliver.

♦ Speak other people's virtues; don't criticize.

Here are some major attributes of leadership that will help insure your success:

♦ The ability to get people to cooperate

♦ Being meticulous and a master of detail

♦ Empathy—the ability to feel what your people are feeling

♦ Decisiveness—making decisions quickly and being slow to change them

♦ Discipline—If you can't control yourself, don't expect anyone to follow you.

♦ Fairness –being willing to do the things you expect of your followers

♦ Accepting responsibility and never blaming

If you always do what you say you're going to do, I can build an empire around you. If you sometimes do what you say you're going to do, you're just another headache for me.

Making your word your bond will make you rare and valuable. I was taught to make my word my bond even if it cost me my last dime. It's not easy, as we're often quick to say we'll do something and then not follow through. We say things like "I'll call you tonight," "I'll send you that list," or " I'll drop over on Saturday" and then don't. The only way to make your word your bond is to limit your commitments. When you occasionally don't do what you say you're going to do, how can anyone know when you will and when you won't? People who don't do what they say they're going to do are nothing more than windbags–in other words, they're full of hot air. What they say has no meaning. If you always do what you say you're going to do, you'll be admired and respected.

You'll have an advantage in business if you realize that for a deal to be a good one, it must be good for both parties. Lots of people want to make one-sided deals, and you'll want to stay clear of them. Good deals generally require a lot of give and take. These are some of the attitudes that lead to success in business and personal life.

Finance

To truly enjoy "the good life" you need to have sufficient funds for your wants and needs. Money doesn't bring happiness, but it sure makes the journey of life more pleasant, and it gives you the chance to help others, which brings great happiness. My friend, Steve Condrey, put it this way: "If you want to have a strong economic position in your later life, you'd better learn to delay gratification in the earlier stages."

It's not how much money you make; it's how much you keep. To have a good financial future you must learn to protect your principal. It's one thing not to make a lot of interest or profit on your investments, but quite another to lose the investment itself. Many people do this by investing in things that are too risky. When something appears to be a great bargain, use an extra dose of caution. *If a deal seems too good to be true, it probably is.* Many of my really poor financial decisions came from investing in deals that seemed too good to be true.

One of the worst mistakes people make is thinking that because something is a certain way today, it will remain that way. The following is a vivid example of how that kind of thinking wiped out many people's finances during the 1980s. Interest rates had been in the area of 9–12 percent for many years, and people were comfortable borrowing money at those rates to buy homes and inventory for their businesses. If you were willing to accept a riskier concept, the variable-rate mortgage or loan allowed you to borrow at lower interest, and on the surface appeared to be a bargain. Over time, these variable-rate mortgages and loans became the norm. With little notice, interest rates began to climb and kept going up until they peaked at 21 percent. Most of the variable mortgages had no limit, or cap, so many people's interest rates more than doubled. Instead of their home mortgage being $3,000 a month, it leapt to $6,000, and there was nothing they could do about it. Since people couldn't keep up with their payments, banks and savings and loan institutions had to foreclose on hundreds of thousands of properties. Once they'd repossessed those properties, the banks and savings and loans couldn't find buyers for them, so many of them began to go broke. Many people lost everything they'd worked their entire lives for, and some became homeless. If someone had said interest rates could go as high as 21 percent, people would have thought they were crazy. Don't let yourself get caught in the trap of thinking things will stay the same.

A more recent example of a sudden, punishing change came after the rise of the stock market as a result of the "technology revolution." Just before it crashed, anyone in the market was making money—generally, lots of it. Dot-com millionaires were being made on a regular basis. Everyone seemed to be a market expert, including people who had never invested in stocks before. People began borrowing money to buy stocks, and invested money they couldn't afford to lose. Then, with little warning, in March 2000 the market started down.

The stocks of many of the world's best known and most respected companies like Microsoft, Sun Microsystems, Oracle, AT&T, Ford, Chrysler, Target, WorldCom, Lucent and Intel — dropped 50 percent or more. First, people lost any profits they'd made, and then they began losing their principal. People who'd borrowed money to buy stocks often had no way of paying it back. Many who thought their stock options had made them rich were left with nothing. This was especially true of those who got in toward the peak of the market. After a steady decline for more than eighteen months, people thought it couldn't get any worse — and then we had the worst terrorist attack in United States history on September 11, 2001. These events prove that the unexpected will happen and you must protect yourself at all times. Limit the money you put into risky investments, and be sure you don't put too many eggs in one basket.

Many if not most Americans live beyond their means. It's a good idea to structure your life so you can live on 80 percent of your net income, and it's an absolute must to save at least 10 percent of what you make. Your savings will insure your future comfort by putting you in a position to let your money work for you. Another good reason to save is to build up a good reserve so you can take advantage of good buys when they come along. *One secret to success in life is to be ready for your opportunity when it comes.*

This is an appropriate place to talk about taxes. Many people get themselves behind the eight ball because of poor tax planning. Taxes are an ongoing fact of life, one that you can look at as the price you pay to drive our highways, have police protection and emergency services, and be protected from invasion by foreign powers. It may seem a lot of money, but we have one of the lowest tax rates in the world, and it's a small price to pay for the freedoms we enjoy. Get in the habit of overestimating your taxes, so you have money left after you pay your tax bill. Avoid having to borrow money to pay your taxes. Accept from the start that you're going to pay what you really owe, because getting in trouble with the government isn't something you want to experience. Be sure to keep good records of your income and expenses, and get yourself a good certified public accountant (CPA). Try your best to plan in such a way that you have no mortgage on your personal residence by age fifty. Get in the habit of estimating your annual income and expenses, and review your total net worth each year to make sure it's going up.

Health

Even though we live in a health-conscious society today, many people still don't practice good eating habits and feel that they're too busy to exercise. Only as you age do you begin to realize the true significance of good health and the fact that very little is possible without it. Good exercise and eating habits give you the best chance for a long, healthy life. There's no question that all of us need to make time to take care of our bodies.

One way to better health is eliminating excesses from your life. Too much of anything is no good. Never smoke, and only drink moderately if at all. Eat to live, and don't indulge just for the sake of taste. Eat little salt and sugar and lots of fresh vegetables.

Be sure you're getting some form of regular exercise, because it's a proven fact that a good exercise program goes a long way toward improving and maintaining your health. Choose a form of exercise you like and stick with it.

Your Thoughts

One of the best books I've ever read on the subject of thoughts is *As a Man Thinketh,* by James Allen. His book, which changed my life, inspired much of what I'll tell you about thoughts. We've discussed the fact that we create our future by our own thoughts, and that our outward life eventually mirrors our thinking. A person who is self-seeking, deceptive, and immoral will lead himself into misfortune. One who is honest, unselfish, and thoughtful will lead himself to happiness, health, and wealth. Your thoughts are your real self, and nearly everything that happens to you is a product of your thinking. If you're happy it's because you have happy thoughts, and if you're sad it's because you indulge in sad thoughts. Knowing this can show you the way to happiness and peace.

People sometimes think of themselves as victims of circumstance, but this is rarely true. Circumstances only control us if we allow them to. If this weren't the case, circumstances would affect all of us the same way. We know that circumstances don't affect all of us the same, because the same event can happen to two people, yet bring about entirely different results. Two people can have the same medical problem, but one gives up and essentially ends life, while the other goes on to achieve greatness. Look at Lance Armstrong, who won the Tour de France after having testicular cancer. This tells us that it's not the circumstance, but the thinking of the individual, that determines the outcome.

In *Think and Grow Rich,* Napoleon Hill shows us how we can use our thinking to achieve anything we want in life. The teachings in his book vastly improved my life, enabling me to go from milkman to owner of my own commercial real estate firm and, finally, to retirement.

When you realize that your future is determined by your thoughts, you see that you must take control of your thoughts. You have to eliminate negative thinking and replace it with thoughts of love, joy, serenity, beauty, and strength. By doing this you become more joyful, loving, and happy. You evaluate others by projecting your own thinking: if you're envious, you see envy in them; if you're a liar you think others lie; if you're trusting, you see others as trustworthy. We usually surround ourselves with others who share our thinking. That's why winners hang out with winners, and losers with losers. Just as birds of a feather flock together, people seek their own kind.

You'll do better in life when you learn to sow good seeds. It's an unfailing law that you reap what you sow. *You can't put your hand in a fire without getting burned.* If you do evil, you'll pay the price. It might not be today or tomorrow, but you will pay the price—Nature always balances her books.

If you fill your mind with goodness, gentleness, love, and compassion, you give yourself good health. If you hold thoughts of anger, hatred, envy, and jealously, you invite grief, despair, and disease into your life. The secret of happiness or misery lies in your thinking. The secret to controlling your outer life is control of your inner life. Once you control your inner life, opportunities will start to come to you. As I improved my inner life, I was amazed at how the right people showed up just when I needed them.

Every moment, you broadcast thoughts that will improve or hurt your life. When you focus on yourself you become your own enemy; when you focus on others you're insuring your own future. Every accomplishment began as a thought. Eventually, you learn to have faith that good will prevail in the end. When you experience fear, worry, doubt, or disappointment, you've lost faith that good will prevail. When you see people who can't retain success, you're seeing people who can't control their thinking and who live in the negative world of self-doubt and self-pity. With a strong purpose and faith in its outcome, you can accomplish almost anything.

One of the first steps to success is developing the ability to control your thoughts through the practice of calmness. Calmness is another rare and invaluable quality. Its opposite is anxiety, and when anxiety steps in, good judgment steps out. To enjoy success, happiness, and peace, it's imperative for you to cultivate a calm and loving attitude, while at the same time eliminating anxiety, fear, and doubt from your life.

The Lesson in a Nutshell

♦ You're now in one of your most productive times, when you're strong physically and mentally.

♦ If you and your spouse chose each other because you're truly best friends, you almost guarantee yourselves a happy future.

♦ A good marriage is a fully integrated partnership.

♦ The cardinal sin in marriage is to think that because your mate loves you, he or she will react to situations and behave the same way you do.

♦ Unsolicited advice and criticism are detrimental to a marriage.

♦ Women usually want the details, and men generally want just the facts.

♦ Most men take things literally, while women often do not — especially when it comes to using words like *always, never, every,* and *none.*

♦ It's a huge mistake to offer your mate the method of caring that *you* want. Find out what your mate wants by asking, and then treat him or her accordingly.

♦ You must learn to "Do unto others as *they* would have you do unto them."

♦ Parenting is one of the least understood responsibilities you face.

♦ Children need and want discipline, and by withholding it you're showing them you don't care.

♦ The fastest way to achieve your goals is to help others achieve theirs.

- Until we like ourselves it's impossible for us to care for others.

- The first step to good mental health is doing the things that make you feel good about yourself.

- Contradict others only if their welfare is at stake.

- One of the highest compliments you can pay anyone is to listen.

- Learn to set the stage for the result you want.

- Often, the attitude you get back from others is like looking in a mirror—they're reflecting your own attitude back to you.

- The only way to get people to do anything is to get them to want to.

- When selecting a career, be sure you're passionate about it, make a good choice as early as possible, and stick to it.

- Whatever you are today is a result of your past thinking.

- When thinking of finance, it's important to remember that it's not how much you make, but how much you keep.

- If something seems too good to be true, it probably is.

- There have been and will be large swings in the economy. It's important to remember this and protect yourself at all times.

- One secret to success is to be ready for your opportunity when it comes.

- Good health should be a priority for each of us, because without it we can't have a good life.

- Calmness is one of life's greatest virtues and rarest qualities.

A Few Profound Thoughts

♦ A wish is a desire without any attempt to attain it.

♦ Who gossips to you will gossip of you.

♦ Nothing causes as much pain as too much pleasure.

♦ The easiest way to get what you want is to help others get what they want.

♦ He who wishes to secure the good of others has already secured his own.

♦ Work twice as hard, expect half as much, and you'll go twice as far.

♦ Quick riches are more dangerous than poverty.

♦ Anything that's wrong gets worse as you delay correcting it.

♦ Some can see at a glance what others cannot see with telescope and microscope.

♦ Choose a job you love and you'll never have to work a day in your life.

♦ To know and not to do is not to know.

♦ Losing is a part of winning.

♦ You're where you are today because of your choices.

♦ Visits always give pleasure, if not in the coming then in the going.

♦ Any person who always feels sorry for himself should.

Lesson Four

Ages 41–54

> *Marriage, Others, Finance, Health, Your*
> *Thoughts, The Lesson in a Nutshell,*
> *A Few Profound Thoughts*

Overview

By the time you're forty-one, you've formed most of the habits that control how you live and the opinions that dominate your thinking. At this point you're approaching the "halftime" of your life. The first thing I'd like for you to consider is that no team thinks of halftime as the end. In sports, the second half is usually the most exciting; it's where the game is determined, and the same is true in life. The first half of our lives prepares us for the rest. Too many people feel that the game is over after age forty, and their fates are sealed. Nothing could be farther from the truth.

You can continue to improve your life as long as you're alive. Have you accepted the fact that your thoughts determine your destiny? This understanding is critical to having a good life, since the only thing that holds you back is your thinking. Once you start truly believing in yourself and eliminate negative thinking, you can make your dreams come true.

These are your "Golden Years," the time you come as close as possible to having it all. Your mental abilities are very strong and you still have good physical health. You've left the excesses of youth behind as maturity has set in, and the aches and pains of old age haven't arrived. This should be an exciting and wondrous time. If you've played your cards right, you now have the funds to live the "good life." If you haven't achieved financial success by now, there's no more time to waste; economics had better become one of your top priorities. It's time to think about and plan for your retirement. Finance takes on its greatest meaning at this stage, so I'll cover it in some detail.

There's nothing you can do about the way you've lived in the past. It's time to take stock of your wants and needs for the future. Begin immediately to do things that will let you live the rest of your life in a way that fulfills your dreams. Get a clear picture today of exactly how you want the rest of your life to turn out. You can still make your wildest dreams come true. Many people didn't achieve economic freedom or greatness until late in life. Look at Colonel Sanders, who, with his Kentucky Fried Chicken, struck it rich in his sixties. Henry Ford and Andrew Carnegie were both over forty before they began to experience their successes.

Abraham Lincoln failed at almost everything he attempted until his late forties.

♦ He was born into poverty in 1809, and at age seven had to work to support his family, who were forced out of their home.

♦ At nine, his mother died.

♦ At twenty-two, he failed in business.

♦ At twenty-three, he ran for the state legislature and lost.

♦ At twenty-four, he lost his job and applied for law school, but was rejected.

♦ At twenty-five, he borrowed money from a friend to begin a business, and in less than a year was bankrupt. He spent the next seventeen years paying off his debt.

♦ At twenty-six, he became engaged, but his sweetheart died. The following year, he had a nervous breakdown and was in bed for six months.

♦ At twenty-eight, he sought to become speaker of the state legislature, but was defeated.

♦ At thirty-one, he sought to become elector, but was defeated.

♦ At thirty-four, he ran for Congress, but lost.

♦ At thirty-nine, he ran for the job of land officer in his home state, but lost.

♦ At forty-five, he ran for the United States Senate, but lost.

♦ At forty-seven, he ran for the vice-presidential nomination of his party, but got fewer than one hundred votes.

♦ At forty-nine, he ran for the Senate again—and lost again.

♦ **At fifty-one, he was elected president of the United States.**

Never think of yourself as being too old to improve and get ahead. Many of life's greatest accomplishments come after the age of forty. You weren't put on this Earth to fail, and a bright future awaits you if you're ready to seize the moment. Good mental health depends on being thankful and appreciative. *It's hard to be sad when you're being thankful.* Too many people focus on what they don't have instead of what they do.

At one time we had season tickets to the Golden State Warriors' basketball games. Our seats were good — about twenty rows from the floor. Game after game, I kept looking at the rows below us, thinking how lucky those people were and wishing we had their seats. During one game, some fans behind us got rowdy, and I stood up and looked back to see what was going on. I was astonished to see that there were seven times as many rows behind us as in front. That was further proof to me that I should appreciate what I had, instead of thinking about what someone else had. Counting your blessings is great for good mental health.

♦ If you woke up this morning with more health than illness, you're more blessed than the million who won't survive this week.

♦ If you've never experienced the dangers of battle, the loneliness of imprisonment, the agony of torture, or the pangs of starvation, you're ahead of 500 million other people.

♦ If you can attend a church meeting without fear of harassment, arrest, torture, or death, you're more blessed than 3 billion others.

♦ If you have food in the refrigerator, clothes on your back, a roof overhead, and a place to sleep, you're richer than 75 percent of the people on Earth.

♦ If you have money in the bank and in your wallet, and spare change in a dish someplace, you're among the top 8 percent of the world's wealthy.

♦ If you can read these words, you're more blessed than the more than 2 billion people in the world who can't read at all.

Marriage

For the last ten years, I've enjoyed a truly happy marriage, and looking back it makes me feel pretty foolish about my previous approach. If you choose to marry, choosing your spouse will be among the most important decisions of your life. Without peace in your home, there's no peace at all. You can't focus on other aspects of life when you don't have harmony with your partner. One of the best ways to improve harmony is with humor. It's one of my wife's greatest assets, and her use of humor helps us have a better relationship. When you're laughing together, the world seems a much better place. You have the most trouble in marriage when you're too serious with each other. Calling one another funny nicknames, acting silly, and being generally lighthearted and playful goes a long way toward a good relationship.

A long time ago I sent Lisa some flowers, and she kept the little card they enclose with the blossoms. This card had a picture of red roses on it, and the words "I love you." One day I opened my desk drawer and there it was. It made me feel great, so I kept it a few days and put it beside Lisa's coffee cup one morning. Next thing I knew, it showed up in a book I was reading. Another day I opened the medicine cabinet and there it was. Ten years later, that worn card is still showing up in different places. It's a fun surprise to get it, and it always says, "I'm thinking about you." You can do the same thing with pictures you like.

Every day, we feed two birds called francolins, which resemble quail and have a high-pitched call. Each morning they come near our bedroom and sound the call to get their birdseed. One silly thing we've found ourselves doing is imitating their call. When one of us comes in the house, or upon getting up in the morning, we often hear one of those silly calls, which makes us laugh and starts our day on a light note. Other things we do include dressing funny or coming out of the bathroom with a goofy hairstyle. Anything you can do to keep each other laughing and the mood light makes a better life.

Many years ago we decided we didn't want any arguing between us. How could we accomplish this goal? We said, "Let's see if we can go one month with no argument". We agreed to work at it and made it happen. Then we said, "Let's see if we can go six months"–and we did. In fact, we've now gone six years. It's encouraging to see how much we can accomplish working as a team. Arguing is no longer an issue, and our lives are richer and less stressful as a result.

One of the main reasons we have such a happy marriage is that we both look out for each other's best interests. We enjoy trying to be the first to unload the dishwasher, make the bed or the coffee, take out the trash, or turn down the bed at night. This attitude keeps us in a mood of caring.

We've increased our happiness by letting each other be who we really are. The tendency in marriage is to try to mold your spouse the way you want him or her to be. This is contradictory to a live-and-let-live attitude. My wife calls her family often, and spends hours on the phone with them. I don't enjoy talking on the phone as much as she does, because I spent twenty-five years on the phone in business. She respects this and lets me act accordingly. My wife also likes to take at least two trips a year to see her family, which I encourage. What would cause a problem would be for her to insist I go along. Trouble usually begins when either spouse tries to impose his or her will on the other. If we're making enough positive deposits in each other's emotional bank accounts, this freedom of choice comes more easily.

These are the years when you're likely to experience your children leaving home. If you haven't had a lot of one-on-one time with your spouse while raising your children, adjusting to

If I'd Known Then What I Know Now

their absence could be a challenging experience. You'll be getting to know your mate all over again in many ways, and it will be more important than ever to allow each other certain freedoms. Since you won't be spending your weekends doing things involving your children, you'll have more time than ever with each other. Don't try to turn your wife or husband into your servant just because you're home more. It should become a mutual benefit to share everything in the extra time.

You can still enjoy a degree of independence. Encourage her to golf or play tennis and to take a trip with her friends once in a while. The two of you probably enjoy some common interests and hobbies. Now you'll have time to learn, or take up a sport you've wanted to share together for years. You can start to plan for your retirement years. This new freedom will allow you to travel the world together and live wherever you choose. It's a new beginning, and you'll want to make the most of it. Now is a good time for the two of you to decide what you really care about and how much is enough. Where and how do you want to live the rest of your lives?

Others

Do you occasionally get down on yourself if you think you're spending too much time pursuing your own happiness? It's entirely normal and healthy to look out for yourself. It's only when you're satisfied with yourself that you can begin to focus on others. Thinking and caring about other people will always be one of the most important means to your success and happiness. Henry Ford said, *"If there's any one secret of success, it lies in the ability to get the other person's point of view and see things from that person's angle as well as your own."* If you want to influence others, there's no better way than to talk about what they want to talk about, seek to understand them, and help them get what they want.

You'll have a huge advantage if you truly want to serve others, because the world is full of self-serving people. By serving others you're really serving yourself, since all you give is given to yourself. If you learn to talk to others about their interests, they'll like and want to be around you. Learn to appeal to their noble sides by saying things like, "I know you'll do the right thing, so I'll leave the decision up to you." One sure way to lose with people is by telling them they're wrong. Show respect for their opinions even if you don't agree with them, and always be quick to admit you might be wrong. Most people have spent too much time trying to prove they're right. If I'd known then what I know now, I'd spend very little time arguing or defending my point of view. It's not that I don't have one; just that I don't need to defend it. This is all part of a live-and-let-live philosophy. Learn to honor other people's thoughts and beliefs. Unless their welfare is at stake, it's best not to contradict them.

You can't avoid dealing with a certain amount of criticism, even though none of us likes it. You know you benefit from constructive criticism, and you can usually accept it if it's given in the right way. Here are some sound rules for dealing with criticism:

Give all criticism in complete privacy.

Preface any criticism with a compliment. There are things about anyone that you can approve, and they need to hear your approval before your criticism.

Criticize the act and not the person. Instead of saying, "The thing I don't like about you is that you always interrupt me," try "I appreciate the suggestions you make when we're discussing things. I find I lose my train of thought however, when I'm interrupted before I finish. Would you be willing to hear me out before offering your suggestions?" You can see that one is aimed at the person, and the other at the act.

Supply the answer. Don't tell someone what's wrong without a suggestion that will correct the situation.

Ask for their cooperation.

Only one criticism per offense. It's discouraging when someone is telling you what bothers him and turns it into a laundry list.

End in a friendly fashion. For example, "Mary, we've been friends for ten years and I admire you for so many things. Thank you for listening to me and being willing to consider my point of view."

Want to or not, you're occasionally going to find yourself in an argument. Avoid arguments whenever possible, because they're a sure way to lose with others. Since some amount of confrontation is unavoidable, here are some of the best ways to deal with it:

Let the other person state his case fully. Drag more out of him or her until they truly have no more to say.

Pause before stating your case. This lets people know you're considering what they said. State your case moderately and accurately.

Be willing to concede something. Don't try to win 100 percent.

Speak through third parties. Instead of saying, "I know very well that this is how it is," try "The other day, I read an article by a man who really knew his stuff, and he said.". Or, say, "On CNN last week, the anchor person made a good point, saying that…" Make it someone else's thought rather than your own and it will be more readily accepted.

Let people save face. You can do this by saying, "I can see how you felt the way you did, and I would have too, given the same information."

Finance

By age forty many of you will be in a position to put your money to work for you. It's often difficult to get a lot of money working for you before then, because your financial needs are generally quite high up to this time. Unfortunately, most people experience their highest expenses prior to earning their greatest income. It will be difficult to earn enough money from wages alone to secure your financial future. One of the best ways to secure your future is through carefully selected, good investments, which can earn you a lot of money—in some cases more than you'll ever make in wages.

If I'd known then what I know now, I'd protect my capital more carefully. It's hard enough to make money and pay taxes on it without throwing it away. Since nearly all investments involve an element of risk, it's a good idea to be sure you've protected your future before making any "risky" investments. Before investing in anything, consider the consequences should you lose the money. If the pain would be too great, don't take the risk. The best investments I've made have been in real estate, and from what I've read and seen, this seems to be true of many wealthy people.

My second-best investment was starting my own business. The third area has been stocks and bonds, and the last venture-capital investment. Before making any investment, it's wise to establish a substantial savings account, setting aside a minimum of six months' living expenses in cash. A logical first investment is your own home. Cars shouldn't be considered an investment, since they depreciate. Assuming you have your minimum of six months' savings in the bank and your home, let's take a look at each of the other investments.

Real Estate

There are several ways to invest in real estate. You can invest in houses or commercial properties, which include warehouses, office properties, retail buildings, and real estate investment trusts (REITs). No matter which type you select, the secret to success is to buy it right. *You make your profit when you buy something, not when you sell it,* and it's a good idea to be a bit fanatical about this concept. One way is by doing the opposite of the masses. When they're buying, you're selling, and when they're selling, you're buying. Real estate runs in cycles, and buying close to the bottom and selling near the top is a sure-fire way of making money. It takes patience and staying power to accomplish this, but it's well worth the effort. The time to buy is as close as possible to the upturn of a cycle. Greed could be your enemy if you try to pick the bottom, as no one knows exactly where a bottom will be.

Here are a few keys to successful buying:

♦ When the real estate market is going up or down, it usually goes in that direction for quite some time. My experience has been that it may last six or seven years. Over time, the real estate trend has almost always been up, providing you buy in the path of progress.

♦ The time to buy is when the masses must sell. Opportunities present themselves when people have to sell because of divorce, death, unemployment, sudden moves because of job changes, and the like.

♦ Cash and the ability to close quickly talk during these times.

♦ Don't fall in love with any particular deal; there are always more.

♦ It's important to remember that buying is easy, but selling is often difficult.

♦ Base your decisions on logic, not on emotion.

♦ Be prepared to walk away from any transaction. *The best bluff is not to be bluffing.* If you say it's your final offer, stick to it.

You'll probably experience fewer problems with commercial real estate than residential. A good investment is commercial real estate with a solid tenant and a triple-net lease. "Triple-net" means the tenant is responsible for taxes, insurance, and maintenance. With a triple-net lease and a credit tenant, all you do is collect the rent. Before you invest in commercial or residential real estate, it's advisable to have a good broker who's knowledgeable in both the properties and the market. If you buy a building or house correctly and keep it rented, you'll not only have monthly cash flow, but also depreciation to help with taxes. Best of all, you'll eventually own the building or house free and clear, as your tenant will pay it off over time. The majority of our income and profits have come from real estate, and it's been the primary contributor to our financial freedom and retirement.

Your Own Business

Starting your own business isn't for everyone: it's very hard work with lots of risk, and many new businesses fail. For the risk-taker with fortitude and desire, this can be an option. Don't even think about starting a business unless you're full of passion about it. When a new business fails it's usually because of insufficient capital, so be sure you have enough money to see you through. Too often, people go into business because they like the type of business, but fail to realize that it can never make them the money they need to live and retire. If you're going to start a business, start one that can meet your financial needs. Be sure to assess the potential net profit. It doesn't matter how much your sales are, it's how much you bottom line. There are businesses that take in a billion dollars a year and lose money. There are also businesses that take in 2 million a year and net half a million.

The main reason the company I founded was successful was that we never lost sight of who were the most important people to the business. We honestly cared about and looked out for the people who worked for our company. They were our priority, and we made sure they were well paid, treated fairly, and their needs were being met. Our ethics and integrity were additional reasons for the company's success. We always did what was best for our people and customers, even when it hurt. The company was founded on those principles in 1974 and began with just a secretary and me. Today it has over three hundred people and offices in three states, and does business all over the world. It's still one of the premier commercial real estate firms in Silicon Valley and in each of the other markets where it has offices. These principles worked for me and they can work for you.

Stocks and Bonds

One of the safest places you can put your money is triple-A-rated, tax-free municipal bonds. You can buy bonds that are both federal and state tax-free. They are for the conservative investor or retired person who doesn't want to risk losing his or her capital.

For the younger, long-term investor, the stock market has proven to be one of the best ways to grow money. Historically, the market has given its investors a 10-percent-plus return. The market always has big ups and downs, so it requires a long- term perspective. If you're a passive investor, I recommend you find and work with a good stockbroker who's committed to your goals. He or she should be insightful and have access to information you won't be willing to spend the time to get. I'm speaking here to the person who is willing to buy and hold good stocks. With a broker, you can't afford to buy and sell stocks very often, due to the commission structure. If you plan to trade a lot, you may be better served to get yourself an online account, where the trades will cost you twenty dollars each or less.

Here are a few suggestions:

♦ Stay away from penny stocks.

♦ Buy stocks that have reasonable price-to-earnings ratios.

♦ Be sure the company has good management, a track record of profits, and is in a business that has a bright future.

♦ Consider selling any stock that goes down more than 30 percent.

♦ Buy only stocks with enough daily volume to be traded at will.

♦ Buy only stocks that don't charge a premium to sell.

♦ Stocks headed up or down usually follow that pattern in the near term.

♦ When a stock has a big run-up, it may be a good idea to backstop it to protect your profit. My experience is that after a big run-up, stocks will usually fall back, offering another buying opportunity.

♦ Trading stocks is risky business and not for the fainthearted.

Venture Capital

Venture capital is a high-risk business with potential for very high returns. If you're going to enter this arena you want the most reputable advisor you can find, one who has a proven track record in venture-capital investing. Only invest money you can afford to lose. Your odds with venture capital are a lot better than in Vegas, but the risk is still great. I got involved with a venture capital firm and invested $100,000. After two years, the firm did quite well and sent me several stocks. Since they helped fund the companies, they received stock warrants, which allowed them to purchase stock when those companies went public. As a result, I received several stocks at different values and quantities. One of them was worth $70 per share at the time, and I received 10,000 shares. Had I sold it immediately, I would have taken a $600,000 profit. The stock looked good, and who knew how high it would go? I didn't sell, and still own the stock. It's currently at 75¢ a share, or $9,000. Clearly, the message is take your profits when you can. Perhaps keep some of the stock for the long run, but always take your profits. Looking back on this I feel foolish; however, I wasn't the first to make this mistake—and I won't be the last. What goes up quickly often comes down quickly. A very wise man once told me, *"Nobody ever went broke making a profit."*

Health

Usually, by this time in your life you've begun to pay more attention to this all-important subject. Thank goodness it's never too late to improve your health. Without good health all the other things that seem so important become secondary. Too often, we take for granted our sight, hearing, and ability to walk and run. It's only when one of them is taken away that we realize their value.

From this point on, an annual physical examination is a must. It's proven that early detection offers the best chance for cure. Your doctor knows the right tests to perform, and this step alone may save your life.

Reading a good book on nutrition and health should be required at an early age, and if you haven't read one yet, don't let another week pass without getting started.

It's vital to find a regular exercise program that fits your schedule. Brisk walking three or four times a week is a good way to start. It's something you can do without having to belong to a health club, and it can be done alone or with your spouse or friends. It's a form of exercise that's actually enjoyable, too. Stretching is very important as we age, and is something you can do anytime you choose—even on the floor while watching the evening news.

Ignorance is no excuse for health problems. Knowledge put to use is the name of the game. You can prevent many health problems simply by acquiring knowledge.

Your Thoughts

When we discussed thoughts in the last lesson, we ended with the idea that calmness was a rare quality and important to our peace of mind. As you gain control of your thoughts, you'll develop an inner peace and confidence you haven't known before. When you gain control of your thoughts, you'll begin to have a clearer view of future events, and better intuition regarding all aspects of life. Control of your thoughts will free you from negative thoughts. You'll be attracted to other people who control their thoughts, and together you'll form bonds that enhance all your futures.

Your success or failure will be determined by the way you control your thoughts. To the degree that you put self aside and focus on others, you'll insure your own future. By focusing all your attention on self, you destroy your chances to succeed or to attract people who'll help you. If you're unselfish, focused and calm, and have a pure heart, you'll set yourself up for success and good health. *One great secret of success is to learn to focus your attention, and hold it where you want it until you've accomplished whatever it is you want.*

Greed is one of our worst enemies, and the greedy person will be a failure no matter how much money he or she has. Many evils come to the greedy, while the generous seem to avoid most of those evils. Learn to be generous with what you have and what you know. Good things are even better when they're shared, and *all you give is given to yourself.* If you're content with what you have, you're rich, and if you're generous with what you have, you're even richer.

It's critical to feed your mind with healthy thoughts and guard carefully what you allow to enter it. Someday we'll teach the importance of our thoughts in schools. We could vastly improve our nation by this one act. Napoleon Hill had it exactly right when he wrote *Think and Grow Rich:* "Anything the mind of man can conceive and believe, it can achieve." We find ourselves surrounded by people who don't understand the importance of their thinking. They allow their minds to be filled with doubt and negativity, and wonder why they fail and are miserable. We are all where we are today because of the thoughts we've let occupy our minds. Your mind eventually takes on the nature of the influences that dominate it. Knowing this, you see how important it is to influence your mind with thoughts that you *want* to be true. The thoughts you allow your mind to dwell upon are a preview of your life's coming attractions. Our thought impulses begin to translate themselves into their physical equivalents almost immediately, whether good or bad.

It's wise to close your mind to people who discourage or depress you. Mind control is the result of self-discipline and habit. Meditation is a powerful way to learn mind control, and to empty and cleanse your mind. Either you learn to control your mind, or it controls you. If you fail to control your own mind, you can be sure you'll control nothing else.

The final concept I want to introduce here was taught to me by a man named Toby Hecht, and is called "Integrity of Self." When it comes to our thinking, happiness, and peace of mind, it's important to understand integrity of self. Evaluate yourself by asking, "Do I act on the things I say I care about?" For example, the person who says he cares about family, but works sixteen hours a day and sees little of his family, is not displaying integrity of self. To have integrity of self in regard to the things we say we care about, our actions must match our words. By acting on what we say we care about, we receive peace of mind. It's vital that we act on the things we say we care about.

The Lesson in a Nutshell

♦ You're only at the midpoint of life; keep setting goals and dreaming, so you can make your dreams come true.

♦ Family traditions are very important: if your family has them, be sure to carry them on; if it doesn't, be the one who starts them.

♦ No joy in life can compare with a happy marriage.

♦ Humor goes a long way toward helping a marriage. Make each other laugh every day.

♦ One way to keep a marriage healthy is by eliminating criticism.

♦ Much happiness comes from being on good terms with *others*.

♦ Learn the seven rules for dealing with criticism.

♦ Learn the five rules for dealing with arguments.

♦ When dealing with finance, protect your capital.

♦ It's easier to make money than to keep it.

♦ If a deal looks too good to be true, it probably is.

♦ From this point on, consider your health a priority.

♦ You are the person you are today because of what you've thought about in the past, your current thinking is your pre-view of your life's coming attractions. Be very careful what thoughts you allow into your mind.

♦ Integrity of self is when your actions reflect what you say you care about.

A Few Profound Thoughts

♦ The things that hurt instruct.

♦ To reap praise you must sow the seeds, gentle words and useful deeds.

♦ Progress includes risk. You can't steal second base keeping one foot on first.

♦ It's easier to resist the first desire than to try to satisfy all that follow.

♦ If you're content, you have enough; if you're complaining, you have too much.

♦ People who talk only of themselves think only of themselves.

♦ A man convinced against his will is of the same opinion still.

♦ If you look to others for fulfillment, you'll never be fulfilled.

♦ Speculate more and know less.

♦ The more you do of what you've done, the more you'll have of what you've got.

♦ Great minds discuss ideas, average minds discuss events, and small minds discuss people.

♦ Live a good and honorable life; then, when you get older and look back on it, you'll be able to enjoy it a second time.

♦ You have reached middle age when all you exercise is caution.

♦ Wise men don't need to prove their point; people who need to prove their point are not wise.

♦ We see things not as they are but as *we* are.

Lesson Five

Ages 55 and Over

*Family, Marriage, Others, Finance, Health, Your
Thoughts, Some Thoughts on Aging,
A Few Profound Thoughts*

Overview

I've spent a lot of time with people much older than
I and have read several good books written by individuals in
their later years. I learned a lot about aging from both, and will
share that information with you in this final lesson.

The quality of our lives in our later years is determined in
large degree by how we have lived until that point. Those who
chose to smoke often pay a heavy price in later life with lung
cancer and breathing disorders. Those who made the choice
to remain overweight often suffer from heart disease, high blood
pressure, and other ailments. Those who overindulged in alcohol often suffer liver problems and ruined relationships. Those
who didn't save for the future don't have the opportunity to
retire. Our lives are all about the choices we make, and the
consequences of each choice.

I've heard many people say that the so-called "Golden Years" aren't so golden. That may be true, but in many cases the reason lies in the way that person chose to live earlier in life. Helping you avoid costly mistakes was my main reason for writing this book. I wanted to provide help to those who wanted a better life and were willing to hear and follow sound advice. Even if you're over fifty-five, you can still make choices that will improve your future. The truth is, you're never too old to start improving your life. It's never to late to begin exercising, eating more healthfully, and improving your habits and relationships. It can be just as rewarding to do it now as when you were younger, and in some ways more. The good life is created by small attempts repeated. Inch by inch, it really is a cinch.

I didn't play golf seriously until I was in my thirties. If you've played, you know it's difficult and takes a lot of patience, practice, and skill to shoot a low score. Because of staying physically fit and being committed to practice, I'm playing the best golf of my life in my late fifties, actually shooting in the seventies often, and occasionally under par. I share this story to give you hope for whatever it is you want to accomplish during the balance of your life. It's not too late to go to college, write a book, become an artist, or do anything else you want to do—if you have the passion.

My life has gotten better year after year, and I have good reason to believe the future still holds better times than the past. These are the years when you can do as you wish. You can speak your truths and not be concerned about how others might judge you. You can wake up when you please and take all the time you want to start your day. You can do all the things you've wanted to do and not have to rush. Everything we do in life takes on new meaning when we have time to do it right, in a hurry-free manner.

If I'd Known Then What I Know Now

Family

Family has taken on its most significant meaning to me in the past few years. The more time I've had to reflect on family, the more I realize its importance. One art everyone should practice is the art of reflection. It's good to look back on your life and remember the events and people that helped you become who you are. When you reflect, you realize how much help you've had along the way and how meaningful your family's support has been.

By the time you reach this stage you're often in a position to offer financial aid. Helping family members can provide a lot of satisfaction. Ironically, you seem to have the most money when you have the fewest needs. To lend a helping hand to a young person is a precious gift. I'm very grateful to those who helped me and want to return the favor by helping others.

One idea that could mean a lot to your family is to document their history. I did this for one of my mentors and it turned out a blessing to them, their families, and me. Documenting your family's history provides a permanent record for future generations of those who lived before them. To sit with a great-grandfather or aunt and have them tell you the story of their life and document it is a rewarding experience. The idea is to provide a permanent record of your heritage.

These are years that allow you to get to know your own children in a more special way, and also offer you the blessing of spending time with your grandchildren. There's no question that you see and think about children differently during these years than when you were younger.

Marriage

Hopefully, by the time you're fifty-five, you're with the person with whom you want spend the rest of your life. Much of the joy in life comes from being with that special someone. Helping your spouse and making each other laugh is good for the soul. My wife and I have progressed in our marriage to the point that we have little, if any, conflict, and neither of us would have it any other way. We both work hard at understanding the other's point of view and not being attached to our own. It gives me pleasure to help my wife whenever I can, and I enjoy really listening when she has something on her mind. We make much better decisions when we discuss things, and I always learn something by hearing her point of view.

A married couple working as a team can be more effective in helping others than either could independently. There's some magic in having both the male and female touch when handling most situations.

It seems much harder dealing with chaos and conflict since I reached age fifty-five. I cherish quiet and being around Nature more. I find my decision making much improved when I have lots of quiet time to think and reflect before arriving at a decision. It seems that the more peace we have in our lives, the better we treat each other and the better our marriage.

Others

This subject holds its importance all our lives. Your success from a very early age depends on your ability to relate successfully with your fellow man. Perhaps your most meaningful time with others comes in this chapter of your life, when you should have plenty of time to give and can share what you've learned and earned. Your income might be more than you need

If I'd Known Then What I Know Now

now, and your wants should be at their lowest point, as you're fulfilled in ways that don't have dollar signs in front of them.

If you've been financially successful, you probably had lots of help along the way. Do you remember how good it felt when someone gave you a helping hand? Now you have the opportunity to be that helping hand. You can help by sharing your wisdom with a young person, or sharing some of the things you don't use or need any more. One of my mentors gave me a set of his favorite cuff links, which I wore with great pride. I've passed them on to one of my sons and told him the story of how I got them. You might want to help a youngster with college or acquiring his or her first home or car. Maybe you want to visit a rest home or children's hospital and cheer up those who can't get out anymore. There are countless ways you can help and be useful. There's not a living soul who doesn't have something worthwhile to offer someone they love or someone less fortunate. The worst thing you can do is sit around and think only of yourself. No joy, peace, or happiness comes from self-seeking.

Giving unsolicited advice is a bad habit. It's one thing to help those who ask for help, and quite another to offer unwanted advice. There are two times to offer advice: the first is when you're asked, and the other is when you see someone in harm's way.

Finance

Finance has taken on new meaning since my wife and I retired. We can't stand the thought of having to go back to work, so we must really take care of what we've saved. When you retire, you need enough money to last you the rest of your life. You might want to have enough to leave something to your heirs. *Making money is one thing; keeping it is quite another.* The United States has just experienced the largest stock-market decline since the Great Depression. A lot of people who had retired are having to go back to work, and many who thought they were going to retire no longer have the funds and must keep on working. When you've saved enough money to retire, you must protect your principal at all cost. It's best to invest your funds in something safe, like government securities or municipal bonds. Put only a small portion in the stock market, and only in very high-quality stocks. It's not wise to put too many of your eggs in the same basket. Diversity and balancing your assets is the name of the game.

Having a good estate plan is a must. There's no need to give the government everything you've worked so hard to acquire. Good estate planning can save you a great deal of money and allow you to leave more to your heirs. Regarding your will, leaving a life estate is an idea worth considering. One of my mentors did this for me, and it's had quite an impact on my life. Each month, when I get my check, I look at a picture of my mentor and thank him for his generosity. Instead of leaving lump sums, we're leaving life estates for some of our heirs. A life estate allows you to give your heirs the portion of your estate you want them to have on a monthly or quarterly basis for the rest of their lives. This gives your heirs their money throughout their lives so they don't risk losing it all at once. It also gives you the ability to bequeath any principal that's left at their deaths to the charity of your choice. I'm a big believer in life estates, and you might find they suit your goals as well. I advise reviewing your will annually—you'll be surprised at how much your thinking changes in that short period of time.

If I'd Known Then What I Know Now

Health

As you get older, being more careful is critical. You've probably noticed how much longer it takes to heal an injury than it did in your younger days. If you choose to throw a ball with a grandchild or play any physical game, you must realize you're not twenty-one anymore. I've paid a heavy price each time I got too excited and overdid my play. The same is true when you do regular exercise. If you're anything like me, you want to lift as much weight or run as fast as you did when you were younger. Moderation at this stage has proven a much better choice. Even small things, like walking up and down stairs, can be dangerous, as you don't have the reflexes you had when you were younger.

When it comes to better health, there's no substitute for exercise. It's something you can do alone and it helps the mind as well as the body. Exercise habits are a good example of using the idea that small attempts repeated will complete any undertaking. Even if you start out doing a half-mile walk, you'll find you get stronger each time, and the first thing you know, you'll be able to walk farther. A few sit-ups, push-ups, or jumping jacks work the same way. Once you start making exercise a habit, you'll do it all the days of your life. In addition to better health, exercise is a great help with weight control.

Your Thoughts

This could be the time when you do the best thinking of your entire life. There's no substitute for combining maturity and experience to get a good result. Our bodies might not be getting stronger, but our minds are possibly at their best. The difference between those who are happy and prosperous and those who are sad lies in the difference between their thinking.

Many seniors complain of boredom; it's a mystery to me how anyone can be bored today with all the options available. Haven't you found that people who are bored are often boring? If you're bored, consider becoming computer literate. It seems sinful to live in the information age without being computer literate. The computer can open up new worlds for you, giving you instant access to information on any subject. You can learn how to garden, find new recipes, and learn about art, music, and health issues. It's the best way to communicate since the telephone. E-mail messages are better than postal mail: they're instant, don't require stamps, and can be sent night or day, seven days a week. Shopping by computer is fast, with no rude salespeople or parking problems. You can do all your research and shopping on your computer. Learning how to use one can eliminate a lot of boredom, and can change your thinking, too.

You're never too old to learn and to investigate things you're curious about. Be adventurous enough to go to places you want to see. You can learn to play golf, to play an instrument, paint, or garden at almost any age. I took up open-wheel auto racing at age forty-nine and it was a great experience. Going to the United States Racing Nationals was a real eye-opener for me. This event was open to all comers, and the Formula Atlantic division had a driver who was *seventy-four years old.* Formula Atlantics are open-wheel cars that look like the ones you see at Indianapolis. They run at speeds exceeding 170 mph. During practice, that seventy-four-year-old had a hard time getting in and out of his car, and I wondered how he could compete. He not only competed, but also won the national title!

The Iron Man Triathlon is held where we live on the "Big Island" of Hawaii. It includes a two-mile swim, a 112-mile bicycle ride, and a twenty-six-mile run. This year, a man in his seventies and a woman in her sixties completed the race. Each did more than twelve uninterrupted hours of demanding exercise to finish the event. Think about these people the next time you think you're too old to do something.

Many seniors indulge in the bad habit of talking about their problems. Talking about your problems won't solve them, and who wants to listen? I remember once in business when one of our salepeople was telling his customer of a problem the customer said to him, "I have my own problems." We all have our own problems and our own aches and pains. What could be worse than listening to someone carry on about his or her woes? Unless you're looking for a solution, keep your problems to yourself. Talking about them just for the sake of conversation just makes it worse for all concerned.

Some Thoughts on Aging

Each of you will want to learn to age gracefully. People often resent aging, instead of realizing that it's a blessing compared to the alternative. You can enjoy the indulgences you've earned by slowing down and turning the race into a walk. As seniors you're freed to do and say almost anything. Instead of fretting about what you've lost, focus on what you still have. When you can no longer do something, replace it with something you can still do. If you can't run, maybe you can walk. Learn to let nature take its course.

You need to keep purpose and meaning in your life by having dreams and goals. Remember that being alone isn't the same as being lonely. It takes grit to suffer your pain silently so as not to burden others. Think less about what's good or bad and simply embrace life as it comes. Learn to become indifferent to things that don't really matter. Time is running out so, be more careful with the time you have left. As you age, keep your mind open to things you might have rejected in the past.

One way to stay healthy mentally is to always be thankful that things are no worse than they are. There are always people with bigger problems than yours. There are no simple answers, and as you age you should realize how little you really know. What you don't know far exceeds anything you'll ever know. With age your humility should grow.

There are some benefits to growing old:

♦ Things you buy now probably won't wear out.

♦ You can live without sex, but not without glasses.

♦ Your investment in health insurance is about to pay off.

♦ Your secrets are safe with your friends now, because they can't remember them either.

♦ In a hostage situation, you're likely to be released first.

♦ You're expected to go to sleep in your chair.

As a wise old man replied when asked how he felt on his ninetieth birthday, " I feel great—except for an occasional heart attack."

A Few Profound Thoughts

♦ Memories of love never pass. They linger, guide, and influence long after the source of stimulation has faded.

♦ It's all right to be content with what you have, but never with what you are.

♦ Things turn out best for the people who make the best of the way things turn out.

♦ The best classroom in the world is at the feet of an elderly person.

♦ Keep your words soft and tender, for tomorrow you might have to eat them.

♦ If people accept your assessment, they modify their actions.

♦ We should continually challenge our strongest beliefs, opinions, and prejudices.

♦ When prosperity was well mounted, she turned loose of the bridle and tumbled out of the saddle.

♦ When a man gets too old to set a bad example, he starts giving good advice.

♦ A person is not old until regrets take the place of dreams.

The Six Most Meaningful
Books I've Ever Read

♦ *Think and Grow Rich*, by Napoleon Hill

♦ *How to Have Confidence and Power In Dealing With People*, by Les Giblin

♦ *As a Man Thinketh*, by James Allen

♦ *The Four Agreements*, by Miguel Ruiz

♦ *The Power of Now*, by Eckhart Tolle

♦ *The Greatest Salesman in the World*, by Og Mandino

Conclusion

I can't understand why so many people fail to *act* when they learn things that will add to their success and happiness. This entire book is based on the premise that you will take intelligent action when you learn something that will help you. There's a world of difference between knowing and doing. To know and not to do is not to know. To benefit from the time you've taken with this book, you must now act.

What's the difference between those who succeed and those who fail? Successful people are willing to do the things unsuccessful people are unwilling to do. It takes self-discipline to succeed, and that means you must be able to give yourself an order and then follow through on it. Self-discipline must become a habit. There's no question that you have it in you to make the moves that will insure your success. The question is, will you be motivated by pleasure-seeking acts or goal-achieving ones? Regardless of what your current habits are, you can change them. To change a habit you must replace it with another. The way to change your habits is to adopt the mindset that small attempts repeated will complete any undertaking. Begin with small goals and get the feeling of small successes. As you achieve a goal you'll feel good about yourself and can set higher goals. Make sure you always put your goals in writing, that they are believable by you, and that they include a definite time for completion.

A journey of a thousand miles really does begin with a single step. That first step often seems trivial, yet it's the seed from which all others will grow. When I sat down and began writing the first words of this book, it seemed a daunting task. By doing a little each day it began to take shape. Then it became pleasant to work on, and now, over three years later, here I am at the end. It's the same for any goal you have for your life.

I've had lots of help in my life, and this is one of my efforts to give back. I hope you've enjoyed and benefited from reading my book, and will use it as a guide to help you and others along life's path. Benjamin Franklin said, "Don't wait for your ship to come in, swim out to it." No matter what the task or goal, grab the bull by the horns and act. May your dreams come true, and may we learn to love and help one another and live in peace.

Wishing you all the best.

J. R. Parrish

ORDER FORM

IF I'D KNOWN THEN WHAT I KNOW NOW
by J. R. Parrish

✍ NO. OF BOOKS ORDERED @ $12.95 EACH	SUBTOTAL ☞
◯ *Please put me on your book catalog mailing list.*	7.25% sales tax (CA residents only)
Shipping & handling charges: $3.00 USPS or $5.00 UPS or priority mail, plus $1.00 for each additional book.	Shipping & handling
Name	TOTAL
Address	Ship to
City State Zip	Address
◯ Check enclosed *Charge to*: ◯ VISA ◯ MasterCard	City State Zip
Card Number	Expiration Date
Authorized Cardholder Signature	Daytime Phone Number

SEND YOUR ORDER TO:

Cypress House
155 Cypress Street • Fort Bragg, CA 95437
or call **1-800-773-7782**
You can also fax your credit card order to 707-964-7531
or visit our website at **www.cypresshouse.com**